"An invaluable book for anyone who seeks to be introduced to the causes of female homosexuality. The candid stories of the multitude of women interviewed by Anne will offer encouragement and hope to the many other women in our midst who struggle with same-sex attractions."

—Janelle M. Hallman, MA
Licensed professional counselor and
international speaker on female homosexuality

"Finally, a contemporary book on lesbianism! I very highly recommend Anne Paulk's insightful and captivating book, which not only recounts Anne's own experiences but offers a window into the lives of many other strugglers. An absolute 'must read' for counselors, religious leaders and every woman who doesn't want to be gay!"

—Joseph Nicolosi, Ph.D.
President, National Association of Research and Therapy of
Homosexuality; author of *Reparative Therapy of Male Homosexuality*

"A great handbook for those struggling with their sexual identity and for anyone who would like to understand the sin of homosexuality in women....I would urge pastors and women's ministry leaders to read this book so they can deal intelligently with women in the church as well as young women confused by our culture."

—Kim Hill
Recording artist, worship leader

"Never has there been a more excellently written and comprehensive *book* on the issues surrounding female homosexuality. I believe this is the most important resource for anyone affected by lesbianism."

—Alan Chambers
Executive Director
Exodus International, NA

"Filled with well-documented research...but the documentation doesn't leave the reader dry, rather it's complemented by real stories that give the human touch....I was reading and hoping that this was a book I could recommend to parents along with women struggling with same sex attractions. I am pleased to say I found that to be true."

—Anita Worthen
Former Exodus Board Member, international speaker,
and author of *Someone I Love Is Gay*

"With all of the confusion today concerning the homosexual lifestyle and its supposed unchangeability, Anne Paulk's new book will be a hopeful eye-opener to many."

—Dr. D. James Kennedy
Senior pastor, Coral Ridge Presbyterian Church
president and founder of Coral Ridge Ministries,
Ft. Lauderdale, Florida

"A masterful work about our sexual identity as women. Clear...comprehensive...scriptural...solidly affirming. This book offers more than hope—it offers healing!"

—Jan Frank
Therapist, speaker, and coauthor of *Unclaimed Baggage: Dealing with the Past on Your Way to a Stronger Marriage.*

Restoring
Sexual Identity

ANNE
PAULK

HARVEST HOUSE™ PUBLISHERS

EUGENE, OREGON

Cover by Koechel Peterson & Associates, Inc., Minneapolis, Minnesota

RESTORING SEXUAL IDENTITY
Copyright © 2003 by Anne Paulk
Published by Harvest House Publishers
Eugene, Oregon 97402

Library of Congress Cataloging-in-Publication Data
   Paulk, Anne, 1963-
    Restoring sexual identity / Anne Paulk.
      p. cm.
   Includes bibliographical references.
    ISBN 0-7369-1179-0 (pbk.)
    1. Homosexuality—Religious aspects—Christianity. I. Title.
   BR115.H6P38 2003
   261.8'357663—dc21   2003001994

Printed in the United States of America.

04 05 06 07 08 09 10 11 / DP-KB / 10 9 8 7 6 5 4 3

*This book is lovingly dedicated to four precious men
in my life—my husband, John, and sons,
Timothy, Alexander, and Jordan.
I love you very much.*

*And to the hundreds of women who entrusted me
with their personal stories of struggles with homosexuality.
Thank you for your honesty and vulnerability.*

110705

Acknowledgments

During the four years I took to complete this project, I have relied on the love and generosity of these wonderful individuals:

Don and Diana Schmierer: Your generosity has overwhelmed me and enabled me to see this book become a reality. Many thanks. Bob Davies and Lela Gilbert: Thank you for the endless hours you both spent poring over my manuscript and enhancing my writing with your skill, advice, and experience.

I am grateful for the expertise, counsel, and friendship of each of my survey reviewers: Bob Davies, Anita Worthen, Jane Boyer, Mary Heathman, Penny Dalton, Brad Sargent, and professional therapists Dr. Joseph Nicolosi, Joe Dallas, Janelle Hallman, and Jan Frank.

My thanks to Focus on the Family president, Dr. James C. Dobson. Your support of my husband and me and your dedication to the truth that men and women can indeed be set free from homosexuality have kept us going through tumultuous times.

The support of my friends at Focus on the Family has helped this become a more significant project: the Love Won Out team, Janet Parshall, Carrie Earll, Suzie Reiple, Sherri Newell, Julie Neils, John McKeever, and Katy Vorce, who provided invaluable assistance in editing and improving my survey—thank you. Paul Pope also provided his expertise in the area of statistical analysis and built the program to evaluate the results of my survey.

Thanks also to my friends and family who encouraged, listened, and were as enthused as I was about this four-year project: Lori Leander, Steve Donaldson, Julie Cole, Jakii Edwards, Dawn Killion, Sandy Hooten, Chuck and Ione Bohler, Robin Stone, Victoria Dillon, Jane Boyer, Amy Tracy, Ann Phillips, Christine Sneeringer, Gloria Zwinggi, Jason Thompson, the staff from Regeneration Books, DeeDee Pitzer, Wendy, Al, and Amy Newill, Eileen Marx, Diane and Sarah Ingolia, and Jim and Jean Daly. Jim, thanks for constantly sharing your enthusiasm with potential publishers as well.

From the first, Nick Harrison at Harvest House Publishers was wonderfully interested in publishing this manuscript. My thanks also to Carolyn McCready and the publisher's committee for your vote of confidence.

When the actual writing portion of this project began in 2002, my husband, John, and my sons, Timmy and Alex, spent dozens of weekends alone as I spent time at a local hotel typing away. Your sacrifice and stress during those long days without me is truly appreciated. I completed the last chapter of this book two weeks before delivering my third son, Jordan Oglesby Paulk, on November 5, 2002. I was a pregnant lady on a mission!

Finally, I remember praying years ago to be of service to my Lord's kingdom in a custom-designed way. Thank you, my God, for taking this vessel of clay and counting me not only your servant but also your daughter and friend. May You be pleased with this book.

Contents

*H*ope for the *J*ourney

*I*n 1982, I embarked on a journey that would shape the rest of my life. Like most journeys, it included a few unexpected curves and valleys along the way. Yet little did I know—nor could I envision—where the adventure would lead me just two decades later. I could not have guessed that I would marry and have a family, be surrounded by many quality women friends, and be so fulfilled as a stay-at-home mom.

With each passing year, I marvel at the work God has done and is still doing in my life. The rewards of this journey— peace, joy, security, contentment, friendships, and rich family relationships—have far outweighed the challenges. My former life seems like a barren wilderness when compared to the lush landscape of my life now.

Very early in my life, I felt the tug of sexual attraction toward some women. I remember being both confused and excited by these feelings and also very unsure of what to do with them. In college, after many years of attraction to other women, I embraced a lesbian identity and lifestyle. A short time later, after an encounter with God, I began my journey out of homosexuality.

Along this road, I've had the company of pastors, friends, and family. Some of them may not have known quite what to do with me, but all were good companions nonetheless. Fortunately for me, I eventually found other women on the same road, walked alongside them, and gained courage and understanding from their companionship. I then realized I wasn't alone. Together we wondered what this new life held for us and asked ourselves if the results would be worth the price we were paying. You may be wondering the same thing.

Or you may be a friend, family member, or support person (such as a pastor, a lay, or professional counselor) of a woman who is struggling with her sexual identity. You may be considering how you can best help her as she makes her way through the maze of sometimes contradictory advice.

Be assured, your support is important. Those of us making the unpopular decision to leave the homosexual life often find a great deal of opposition and very little encouragement. Some women must leave behind a way of life that has seemed inescapable and a community of like-minded women who represented their entire support system.

On the following pages you will read stories from many women making this same journey out of lesbianism. Because of the intimate nature of this topic, most of the stories are compilations and do not represent any particular individual. You may find some of the experiences are remarkably like your own, others less so. You may also identify with some of the results of a survey I conducted of 265 women who had left the lesbian lifestyle. These are women who have made that all-important decision to take the journey toward wholeness.

Years ago I was looking for help as I left lesbianism but found almost no resources. Fortunately, I was referred to a wonderful Christian counselor willing to help me work toward my goal. A few years later, I found out about Exodus International, a Christian organization helping individuals leave homosexuality behind. At Exodus, I found others who had felt the tug of same-sex attraction but were experiencing real change. The hope I've found has motivated me to share in this book what I have learned and experienced.

Finally, I don't know how this book has come into your hands at this particular time. But if it has come as a gift from a friend or relative who loves you, my prayer is that you will be open to the potential for change in your life.

If you're reading the book because you have a friend or relative struggling with lesbianism, my goal is to help you understand more fully the daily struggle your loved one faces.

For those of you reading this because you're already on the road to restoration as a woman, my hope is that through these pages you will find great encouragement.

You are not alone in the journey.

Three Stories

A few years ago Focus on the Family, the large ministry with whom my husband, John, and I are associated, designed a one-day conference on homosexuality they hoped to take to several large cities around the country. John, who was heading up this new program called Love Won Out, began calling pastors in one large northwestern metropolitan area, looking for a church to host the first conference.

Much to everyone's dismay (and surprise), John placed 25 phone calls before he found a pastor willing to sponsor the event.

Now, only a few years later, Love Won Out has a waiting list of churches nationwide who want to host a conference. Interest in homosexual issues has exploded in Christian circles in a short time. Perhaps this newfound attention is a result of the increased visibility of homosexual activists. Perhaps it's caused by the outspokenness of ex-gays who have talked publicly about their own struggles with same-sex attractions in hopes of helping other strugglers. Or it might be due in part to men and women who have secretly wrestled with their sexual identity, hoping for the possibility of change. Also, concerned friends and relatives want to learn how to cope with the news that someone they love is a homosexual. As a result, wherever John or I speak, we meet people with questions about their own sexuality or that of someone they care for. Because of my own personal history, women often confide in me. Typical of those I've met are the three women whose stories follow: Megan, Taylor, and Christina.

Megan's Affairs of the Heart

I met Megan, a young 28-year-old Christian woman, through a mutual friend. After discovering my ministry to women struggling with same-sex attraction, she pulled me aside and asked if we could talk. With great emotion, Megan told me she had been pleading with God, *Please, Lord, remove these overwhelming feelings I have toward other women. I don't understand why I have to go through this agony! Why won't my sexual temptations toward women just go away?*

Megan had felt attracted to other females off and on since she was 14 years old. To her credit she had not acted on those feelings even though she was heavily tempted twice. Instead she "white-knuckled it" until her feelings passed or the tempting friendship came to a close. At times the struggle was so difficult she wondered if she would make it without expressing her feelings some way or another.

One particularly difficult relationship took place in high school. Megan had gotten to know Vanessa, a confident, beautiful girl and a strong Christian. By contrast, Megan said, "I sat next to Vanessa quietly in class, afraid I might push her away somehow. Soon I began to express only the parts of me that I knew Vanessa liked—my sense of humor, for example— and I stopped doing things that didn't interest Vanessa. I became one-dimensional."

Megan recounted watching as boys vied for Vanessa's attention but hardly seemed to notice her. During visits to Vanessa's home, Megan felt warmly welcomed and included in Vanessa's inner circle of friends. All day long Megan thought about Vanessa, fantasizing about an exclusive relationship and physical touch between them. She looked forward to spending time with Vanessa just to get the hugs at the beginning and end of each visit. Eventually Megan's personality had disappeared so much that Vanessa lost interest in her. Megan's unique qualities and independent identity had been traded for closeness with Vanessa. Vanessa had become more than an object of admiration—she had become like an idol.

When Megan attended a Christian college, her endurance was tested all the more. During her sophomore year, she became "best friends" with Amy, a fellow nursing student. The two young women did everything together, but a physical temptation didn't surface until one day when Amy made a romantic gesture toward Megan. In that moment, Megan remembered a Bible verse she had learned warning against such activity.

> Do you not know that the wicked will not inherit the kingdom of God? Do not be deceived: Neither the sexually immoral nor idolaters nor adulterers nor male prostitutes nor homosexual offenders... will inherit the kingdom of God (1 Corinthians 6:9-10).

Instantly Megan felt the guilt of her attraction toward Amy. *How could I do this to You, my God?* Megan thought to herself. As a result, she rejected Amy's overture and the two resumed their nonsexual friendship. For the time being Megan felt safe.

Megan didn't know what caused or fueled her attraction to other women. She was tortured by the fact that they were even there. She felt as if she couldn't talk to anyone about it—especially Amy.

If only Megan had known that she wasn't alone, that there were others who had successfully faced and overcome feelings just like hers. If only she had felt comfortable bringing to her pastor the struggles that caused her such turmoil. Instead she had received the message that personal weakness, especially in the area of homosexual attraction, would likely be met by an inability to help at best and by labeling and further isolation at worst.

When I asked Megan why she didn't confide in her pastor, she told me she had overheard him telling a condescending joke about homosexuals at a church picnic. How sad that she felt a lack of understanding from a Christian leader who was meant to shepherd her.

Megan said, "I can't go to my pastor. On the other hand, I feel like I can't go to just any counselor either. I have read for years in newspapers and magazines that homosexuality is inborn and that people can't change. So what's the use?"

Interestingly, Megan's friend Amy began attending an ex-gay support group and invited Megan to go with her to a regional Exodus North America conference for individuals seeking freedom from homosexuality. I met Megan at that conference. During several talks we had during the conference, Megan broke out of her silence and isolation for the first time. As we parted when the week was over, I encouraged her to share her concerns with Amy and to think about joining a local support group when she returned home.

Megan knew that change would be difficult, but she was excited about it. She responded to the possibility and began to gain hope, confidence, and freedom as she walked through the next six months alongside brothers and sisters in Christ who knew and understood her struggle.

When we met at another conference less than a year later, Megan shared that she had finally talked with her pastor about her struggles. I asked her what had motivated her to do so.

"I'm so excited about what God is doing in me that I wanted to let him know...just in case others were struggling with same-sex attraction."

"So how did he respond?" I asked.

"Well, his jaw almost dropped," she said, "but he thanked me for my candor. He told me he didn't know a lot about how to help someone with this struggle but was willing to walk alongside me. He said he would read up on the topic and asked me for some good books. So he asked *me* for help!" she exclaimed with a grin.

"That's great!" I said. And then I asked what other discoveries she'd made since I'd seen her.

"Well, let's see..." she began. "This past year I've learned what true accountability is—it's being honest in my small group in the face of attraction, but *not* to the individual to whom I'm attracted. I've also learned that my sexual attraction toward other women is not simply sexual. It's really a measure of emotional insecurity in my life."

"Can you give me an example?" I asked.

"Two months ago," Megan began, "I felt very attracted to a woman at work. I mentioned it to my small group leader, and she asked me what at first seemed to be irrelevant questions. She asked, 'What stresses are you going through right now? What other feelings are you experiencing?'"

"I began to list the changes in my life: a job change, some good friends moving out of state, and my father undergoing surgery the following week. A light bulb went on. I was grasping for some form of security and comfort. My heart told me that if I was in a lesbian relationship with the woman at work, I would feel better—kind of like what I suppose a drink offers an alcoholic."

In just a year, Megan was beginning to understand the triggers that set off her attractions—and how to deal with them appropriately.

Taylor, a Gen-Y Example

One Thursday evening, a young man who attended our high school ministry motioned to me to come pray for a female friend of his. "She's kind of confused right now..." he said. I introduced myself to the young woman, who told me her name was Taylor. Her slumped shoulders and obviously sad disposition told me immediately that something was bothering her.

"How can I pray for you?" I asked.

Taylor could hardly bring herself to raise her head and look at me to answer. She was clearly depressed, and yet I wondered how I could help. She was an extremely attractive blonde, dressed nicely, and had nothing about her to suggest a homosexual struggle. But she began sharing her problem by telling me, "I'm afraid I might be gay."

"Why do you think that?" I asked.

"Well," Taylor explained, "I've been having recurring dreams that I'm gay."

"Have you ever had an attraction toward another girl or woman when you were awake?" I asked.

"No."

"Are you attracted to boys?" I asked.

"Yes—I always have been."

"Other than your dreams, do you have any other reason for thinking that you might be gay?" I asked.

"Well, no," she answered thoughtfully.

She then explained several influences in her school. The administrators were gay, several of her teachers were openly gay, her textbooks included positive references to homosexuality in many places, the gay and lesbian alliance club had a voice on campus, and, of course, the school provided "tolerance" training. The message Taylor had received was coming through loud and clear—so clear that she began to have dreams that she was gay, even though she had no other basis for questioning her sexuality.

"The teachers can't seem to get enough of it," Taylor concluded. "But if you disagree with them and say that homosexuality isn't right, watch out!"

With that I explained what the Bible had to say about the purpose of sexuality.

"Sex isn't a bad thing, you know. After all, God is the creator of our sexuality and has provided us with boundaries for our emotional, spiritual, and physical protection. He wants what's best for us, and He hates sin because it robs us of the best He has to offer. The marriage relationship between a man and a woman was meant to reflect God's character and His desire to be in fellowship with us."

I waited for Taylor to speak, but she was silent.

"Do you have a personal relationship with this most incredible Person in the universe?" I continued. "You need to know that Jesus is a person who is interested in having a relationship with you. He said: 'Take my yoke upon you and learn from me, for I am gentle and humble in heart, and you will find rest for your souls. For my yoke is easy and my burden is light'" (Matthew 11:29-30).

"Taylor, I think you need to ask Jesus into your heart. But I also want you to know that this is a serious decision. You shouldn't be pushed into it." By then, our pastor's wife had joined us. Together, we showed Taylor several more Scripture verses having to do with becoming a Christian. Finally I asked, "Taylor, would you like to begin a personal relationship with the One who created you?"

"Yes," she replied with calm certainty.

We led Taylor to Christ with a simple prayer. In one incredible moment, this confused young woman passed from one spiritual destiny to another and became an inheritor of eternal life, a daughter of the Great King. Before, she had lived life by her whims and the pressure from her peer group in high school. Now she would begin to live by the principles and precepts of God's Word, which would give meaning and form to her life. She would no longer have to be ruled by the sway of unreliable emotions. She was finally standing on solid ground. Despite the messages her school curriculum, peers, and teachers communicated, her heart had told her something else: Her soul would suffer serious costs and consequences if she followed the path of her fearful dreams.

After the prayer, Taylor's face radiated relief, peace, and confidence. She held her head high, and her eyes smiled confidently. She appeared to almost float out of the room. God had met with Taylor in her heart, had reassured her, and had given her peace and confidence.

A month or so later, I met up with Taylor and asked her how things were going.

"Lately, school has been great," she told me. "I feel so much more self-confident. Not everything has been easy though. My friends noticed something different about me and made fun of my commitment to Jesus. That was really awkward, to be honest."

I also wondered if she had any greater insight about why she had the recurring dreams. When I asked her, Taylor responded: "I haven't really thought about my nightmares for a while, but I think they may have had something to do with the constant discussions, training, books, and everything we hear about homosexuality at school."

Like many others in contemporary society, Taylor's attitudes had been formed—or misinformed—not by reality but by her peers and the influential adults around her.

Christina—A Classic Story

When I met Christina at an Exodus conference, she was living with her female lover of three years, but she confessed, "I'm longing for someone else or something else... I've spent the past three years thinking I had it all: a lifelong relationship, friends, and a good job—but something is missing."

Chris didn't grow up in a Christian home. Her parents married young and didn't get along very well. Their constant fighting often turned into a barrage of angry words, leaving damaged hearts. Chris' mom always seemed to end up losing, or rather, giving up.

"Women!" her dad often said in frustration as he stormed out of the house in a furious whirlwind.

Chris' mom would then be left in a puddle of tears with three small children to care for. Chris, though only a kinder-gartener, was the oldest, and although she hurt for her mother, her little heart was quickly making judgments about all sorts of important things. She remembers deciding after one of the arguments when she was about four, "Daddy is mean to Mommy. I don't want to be weak and get hurt like Mommy." So she separated herself from her mom and began following her dad around. Chris started helping him in the garage, happy to be with him doing anything that had nothing to do with her weak mom. Sometimes she even imagined herself to be a little boy. And so began her tomboy image and her habit of emulating her father.

Because of the difficulty at home, Chris did not get along well with others at school. She was introverted and hard to get to know. She rarely asked questions of her teachers and was awkward with her classmates. "I guess you would have called me a loner," she explained. "I really wanted to laugh and play with the other kids but just felt like I couldn't."

In middle school, at that critical time when puberty hit, Chris felt even lonelier and more isolated. "I just didn't feel like I fit in. Fortunately, I was talented at sports. That gave me an 'in' with certain boys who became my 'buddies.' I liked that, but I felt terrible about being a girl. I also remember despising my mother. She had been such a doormat, never really standing up to my father and stopping his verbal attacks.

"Somehow I always felt as if I was there to comfort, protect, and care for my mother. I was there for her needs, but she wasn't really there for mine. Sometimes I even felt invisible. Our relationship at that time is kind of hard to explain, but that's how I felt. Even when my father left us when I was 15, Mom seemed weak and leaned on me."

In high school, Chris joined the girl's soccer team and continued to find her identity in sports. Through soccer she became friends with several other girls and felt intrigued by them. For the first time, she really had a female group to "hang out with."

"We would do sleepovers at their houses," Chris explained, "but not at mine. I was too embarrassed. One girl, Tammy, was so cool. She really seemed interested in me, and that's when I had my first attraction to a girl."

Chris explained that her friendship with Tammy quickly turned into an exclusive relationship and became sexual. Eventually, Tammy's parents found out and ended the girls' friendship. Both Chris and Tammy felt humiliated. And Chris was alone again.

> That's when I decided I was gay and started going to gay bars. I was only seventeen, but they let me in anyway. I had finally found a bunch of women who loved and accepted me, and it felt good—really good!
>
> I had fun dancing and connecting with other women. Not long after I started going there I met a 25-year-old woman and started dating her. By my eighteenth birthday, I had moved in with her—but it only lasted a year. I was devastated when it ended. After that I had several relationships with other women, but none of them lasted for more than three months.
>
> Now I'm with Karen. We've been together for three years and we're still going strong. She's like

me in that she likes hiking, biking, and stuff like that...and we just bought our first house together. But I'm constantly wondering if I'm missing something. I don't know what's wrong with me. I should be happy. Life is finally good.

"So what seems to be the problem?" I asked.
Chris shook her head in bewilderment.

Well, a couple of years ago, my mom became a Christian. She started sending me verses from the Bible, booklets, and stuff like that. I was angry with her because she seemed so hypocritical. I didn't call her for a year. Then we got into a fight, and I told her how mad I was because she sent me that Christian stuff. I asked her why she thought she had the right to judge me. "Just leave me alone!" I told her. Ever since then, any time Mom calls, she tells me she's praying for Karen and me.

Maybe I came to this conference just to find out if I *am* missing something and to see what Christianity is all about. I thought this would help me to just dismiss the whole thing, but I actually find myself drawn to it somehow.

I explained that she wasn't being drawn to the conference but to God. "The Holy Spirit is calling your heart ever so gently. In Jesus Christ you will find the comfort, safety, and peace you're looking for. He's the only One who can meet all your deepest needs," I quietly explained. "Jesus is the Person we're adoring during each evening meeting. God has done so much for us, generously loving us, that we return His love in song and in the way we live. That's our motivation for getting together during this conference week."

Chris nodded. She didn't seem to have anything else to say.

I met with Chris several times that week, just to catch up. God was intently wooing Chris, and as she attended the workshops and evening worship meetings, He gradually melted her heart. She had been given a new Bible by one of the workshop teachers and excitedly told me she was reading the gospel of John late into the night. All her questions were being answered and dismissed. On the final night of the conference, Chris gave her life to Christ. At last she had found Someone whom she could completely trust—Someone who promised to never leave her or forsake her.

The next few months were difficult. Chris went home to face Karen, her lover, with the news that she had become a Christian. That did *not* make Karen excited!

"She felt betrayed and so did all my lesbian friends," Chris told me. "They just didn't know what to make of me. Soon they didn't want anything to do with me. Karen felt really hurt when I told her that I couldn't sleep with her anymore. Something in me was changing, and I just couldn't do whatever I felt like anymore."

"Chris, the changes going on inside of you are from God, who now lives in you through His Holy Spirit," I reassured her. And then I read to her two verses from the Bible.

> Now it is God who makes both us and you stand firm in Christ. He anointed us, set his seal of ownership on us, and put his Spirit in our hearts as a deposit, guaranteeing what is to come (2 Corinthians 1:21-22).

> So I say, live by the Spirit, and you will not gratify the desires of the sinful nature. For the sinful nature desires what is contrary to the Spirit, and the Spirit what is contrary to the sinful nature. They are in conflict with each other, so that you do not do what you want (Galatians 5:16-17).

"Chris, the Holy Spirit took up residence in your heart when you became a Christian," I said. "And this is an evidence that you really are a Christian. According to Colossians 1:12-14, this now applies to you:

> Giving thanks to the Father, who has qualified you to share in the inheritance of the saints in the kingdom of light. For he has rescued us from the dominion of darkness and brought us into the kingdom of the Son he loves, in whom we have redemption, the forgiveness of sins.

"Chris, you are now a citizen of heaven, an inheritor of the God of all creation, and you naturally want to please the One who gave everything for you. Life will never be the same for you," I told her with a smile.

Over the past several years I've met many women like Chris who make the hard decision to leave their lesbianism behind for the rewards of knowing Christ—and the experience never gets old. Nor does it seem to get any easier. Women who step out of their old life into their new one *will* face some hardship.

The Process of Growing

Megan, Taylor, Christina—each of these women have dramatically different stories with their own unique challenges along the way. Taylor, who only suffered from dreams of being a lesbian, found resolve quickly. But most women facing same-sex attraction—like Megan and Chris—find the process of change just that—a *process*.

A process similar to growing from childhood into adulthood.

My middle son, Alex, recently told me that he *is* a man and a daddy. Those are good aspirations for him, but at two and a half, he has a long way to go to fill those shoes. We, like Alex, aspire for good things but need patience to grow into the women God desires us to be. We want to experience all He has for us *now*, but God uses time as He binds up our wounds, matures us emotionally, and nurtures us along the way. He wants us to be women who are gentle and strong with quiet confidence and maturity.

Megan is just beginning to move past the shame of dealing with same-sex attractions to knowing she's loved and accepted by God regardless of her struggle. She will need to understand and embrace the grace that God has extended to her. She may even have a harder time than Chris in understanding and relying on God's unconditional love for her. What Chris learns by necessity, Megan will fight to obtain. Perhaps she will read with new eyes those verses from 1 Corinthians 6:9-11:

> Do you not know that the wicked will not inherit the kingdom of God? Do not be deceived: Neither the sexually immoral nor idolaters nor adulterers nor male prostitutes nor homosexual offenders nor thieves nor the greedy nor drunkards nor slanderers nor swindlers will inherit the kingdom of God. And that is what some of you were. But you were *washed*, you were *sanctified*, you were *justified* in the name of the Lord Jesus Christ and by the Spirit of our God (italics mine).

Chris needs first and foremost to get to know her Savior and then to work through the hard issues of living in a house with someone who is alternatively hostile and seductive. She will face the problem of separating households and will grieve the loss of her relationship with Karen. She will need to find a new support system and community after being rejected by her old ones.

The Body of Christ is designed to be that support system. Chris has been born into a new family, and in time she will get to know brothers and sisters who have all come out of some form of bondage into the freedom Christ gives.

As Chris, Megan, or any other woman moves along on her journey, she will face many challenges, but in each one, she has the joyful company of Someone who will be infinitely closer than a brother or sister—our Lord Himself.

2

Where Does Same-Sex Attraction Come From?

I had just finished speaking at a church and was about to pack up my notes to leave when I noticed a young woman shyly approaching me.

"Hi," she began. "I'm Nicole." As she introduced herself, I noticed that she was slightly overweight and that her jet-black hair was somewhat unkempt. She was clearly nervous about speaking to me, but as we talked, she eventually opened up.

"Anne, I've become sexually involved with my best friend, and I don't know what to do about it," she confessed. "I asked a woman counselor at my church for help, and she said that I was born gay and that I had better just accept it and move on."

Nicole hesitated and then asked, "Is the counselor right? Was I born gay?"

I spent the next several minutes trying to answer her important question—one that I'm frequently asked. It's a complicated subject, to be sure. And to answer it in the best possible way, I like to separate it into three parts:

■ First, are women "stuck" in their sexuality?

■ Second, has biological science proven that *anyone* is born gay?

■ Third, if science hasn't proven homosexuality is inborn, what factors could contribute to same-sex attraction?

I will answer the first two questions in this chapter. Chapter 3 is an in-depth consideration of the third question.

Are Women "Stuck" in Their Sexuality?

After talking to hundreds of women during the past several years and hearing their stories of same-sex attraction, I'm convinced the answer to this first important question is no. Some of the women I've talked to have admitted to being attracted to women most of their lives. But I've also talked to women who have been married and otherwise heterosexual yet have found themselves in homosexual relationships.

Still others have shared their stories of childhood experimentation with other girls and the guilt that stills weighs heavily upon them. These women, too, for the most part have gone on to lead heterosexual lives.

I have heard endless variations on similar themes—all of which support the conclusion that a woman's sexuality can be relatively fluid throughout her life. This is evidenced in a survey I conducted in the year 2000 among women coming out of homosexuality.[1] Of the 265 women who responded to the extensive survey, three out of four had engaged in sex with a man. Even more surprising was that three out of five of the surveyed women had sexual relations with a man after having already felt sexually attracted to another female. Later in the survey, I asked unmarried women, "Were you ever sexually involved with a man, even when considering yourself lesbian?" Three out of ten answered that they had been—a behavior that would be unheard of in the gay male community.

The fluidity of female sexuality has been asserted by many researchers. According to feminist writer and teacher Carla Golden, Ph.D.,

> For women, sexuality may be an aspect of identity that is fluid and dynamic as opposed to fixed and invariant. I came to think of women's sexuality in this way as a function of interviews and more general discussions with young college women who were exploring their sexuality.[2]

Even Dr. Dean Hamer, who is a gay activist and biological researcher, agrees. Based on anecdotal evidence he had collected, he concluded, "Women tend to be more sexually fluid. We've interviewed lesbians who have always identified as lesbian but who fantasize about men."[3]

Generation Y and Beyond—Lesbian Experimentation

The newest factor influencing the attitude of younger generations seems to be somewhat unique—an almost constant focus on homosexuality in many forms of media and in schools. I believe that homosexuality's prominence in these places is causing a change in the sexual expression of girls. This first came to my attention through Taylor's fearful dreams, as mentioned in chapter 1. My interviews with high school girls from several states have confirmed this.

For example, I asked Rachael, a 17-year-old Christian girl, how homosexuality impacts her school. Rachael told me she has never struggled with homosexuality but that it comes up in class discussions and casual conversations with her friends. She described one incident this way: "Some girls and guys were eating lunch one day, and my friend Emily asked the guys, 'How much would you pay me to kiss Ally?'" Rachael remembered laughing at the suggestion but was shocked when Emily leaned over and kissed Ally. Rachael immediately got mad at her friend and said, "That's gross!"

What surprised Rachael even more was the rebuke from the other students around the table. Although they were not involved in homosexual behavior themselves, all of the kids verbally jumped on her. She told me, "I felt I wasn't allowed to say why I thought it was wrong. The strange thing was that both the girls involved were straight. Isn't that weird?"

I told Rachael that her friends' actions didn't surprise me and recounted a similar experience I'd had only a few days earlier. Walking to the store with my sons, we passed a group of high schoolers. Two girls were in a group of guys and one of the girls yelled out loud enough for any passersby to hear, "Which one of you guys will pay me $50 to kiss her?" I told Rachael that the girls were just trying to get the attention of the guys.

Rachael nodded, "That's pretty typical."

"So is homosexuality now seen as cool?" I asked.

"No, not really," Rachael responded. "The kids use the word 'gay,' instead of 'stupid.' Girls who play around kissing other girls in high school are seen as cool unless they are really gay. It's usually done in the presence of some guy they're attracted to. Other girls make it a habit of kissing girls as a joke, but I wonder if they aren't more serious about it. Some lesbian girls are seen as cool because of their athletic ability but not because of their sexuality."

After speaking with a half dozen of these young women from different geographic areas, I came to a few conclusions. Girls who were otherwise heterosexual were engaging in lesbian sexuality, possibly for a variety of reasons: trying to get the boys' attention, personal lack of sexual boundaries, no reason to say no, or perhaps as a participant with a girl who was trying to excite a guy. Part of this phenomenon is probably linked to the encouragement of sexual expression by the pornographic magazines that many boys read. But as a result of all this, a whole new generation of young women will need ways to understand these seemingly tame sexual experimentations, realize what these experiences led them to, and learn how to move on into whole, healthy adult relationships. Will they find the right answers?

Childhood Experimentation

Some women still have unresolved feelings about same-sex experiences that took place in their youth. These women struggle with a nagging feeling of guilt, they question their sexuality in adulthood, or they experience unexpected anger toward women and men who identify themselves as homosexual.

Take Mary for example. She walked up to me at a book signing and began pouring out her heart. For Mary, early experimentation with another girl eventually turned into a very personal guilt-racked question: "If I had sexual contact with another girl, does that make me a lesbian?"

I assured her it didn't.

On another occasion, a friend called and began to share some of her pain. Barbara related how a relationship with an older woman had taken a sexual turn.

"Anne, this woman treated me like a daughter," Barbara said. "In fact, I am her daughter's age, and that's one reason we became very close. I really needed the nurturing she was providing, but one night our friendship turned into a more intimate, sexual relationship. I would stay overnight there every once in a while, and we used to sit up late talking after the other kids had gone to bed. The warmth of her words drew me in. I was only 18 years old, but I still feel like the encounters were all my fault. And since then I've wondered, am I homosexual?

"Anne, I love my family so much," Barbara went on. "Every day I am thankful that God has given them to me, but I have this shame, guilt, and anger to deal with. I was wondering if you would help me sort through it."

I answered Barbara's basic questions, but I asked her to follow up on our conversation by meeting with a Christian therapist who could work with her to sort out her feelings of betrayal and guilt.

Barbara is one among many women who have "dabbled" in same-sex sexual experience but have not embraced homosexuality as an identity. Instead, to some degree, their experience was more like water off a duck's back. The identity and lifestyle just didn't fit, so it was discarded. And yet, although they moved on, they still carry baggage from the past—baggage that is heavy, guilt inducing, and shameful. Many of these women say their early same-sex experience "took away" some of the intimacy they longed for in their marriage.

Resolving these feelings of shame is an important step in the restoration process. But not all women are wounded by youthful experimentation. Sometimes their foray into lesbianism comes later, perhaps during a time of stress.

Seemingly "Out of Nowhere" Attraction

Jill found herself in a lesbian relationship by a somewhat surprising turn of events. An intelligent and beautiful woman in her mid-20's, she married a man who was a recent convert to Christianity. They had what looked like a perfect life—a new home, a romantic marriage, and successful businesses. Jill was a talented graphic designer and her husband was in middle management of a high-tech firm. They had the American dream, or so it seemed.

After the birth of their son, Jill struggled to find time for herself. Both Jill and her husband were so busy with the colicky baby that they had little time to care for each other. Jill began going through an identity crisis, longing for the accolades and self-worth that her business success had brought her. None of her friends were aware of her feelings. So instead of getting the friendship support she needed and longed for, she was becoming more and more needy. Her demands for emotional nurturing became exhausting to her husband. The stress was severely testing their commitment to each other while everything looked perfect on the outside.

Then one day, Jill ran into a friend from college. Even though she knew her friend was gay, Jill agreed to accompany her to a lesbian bar. Jill had never seriously been attracted to another woman, but she'd had a very close friendship with another girl in college. She had become aware on one particular evening that her friendship could have become sexual.

Late one evening the two young women were alone, sharing confidences. Jill was feeling a deep need for her friend's consolation because of some difficulties in her life, and she felt the tug of wanting to be wrapped up in her friend Tammy's arms. But her thoughts went beyond that for a moment. When the mood changed and Tammy was ready to leave, Jill discarded the feelings by telling herself they were simply a momentary lapse. So Jill had experienced same-sex attraction before, yet she had never admitted it to herself or anyone else.

Now in her struggling marriage, she once again faced tangled emotions that were threatening to overwhelm her. When the other college friend asked her to go out for the evening, she decided that enjoying a light-hearted night out would be entertaining. *A good diversion,* she convinced herself. But her beauty caught the eyes of many of the lesbian women. The attention felt good to her even though it was from women.

Before long she revisited the lesbian bar with her friend. Jill was becoming captivated by the admiration given her as the token "straight" woman. Some dormant feelings were awakening because of the company she was keeping at the bars.

Eventually, after numerous chance meetings with lesbian women outside the "bar scene," Jill was becoming more and more attracted to their adoration and attention. She began returning the flirtations. She sensed a profound contrast between the frustrations of her world at home and the powerful feelings of nurture she received elsewhere. She liked feeling attractive and wanted by the lesbian world, and eventually the temptation was too much for her. She found herself fantasizing about being cared for by another woman and participating in a sexual relationship with one particular lesbian, Samantha. Fantasy led to flirtation and then on to the exhilarating rush of allowing "Sam" to pursue her. After months of living what had become a double life, Jill decided to leave her husband and young son for Samantha.

Sadly, Jill's experience is not altogether unique. Films have been produced and books written about this very dynamic—the unfulfilled, under-appreciated housewife who becomes open to an adulterous affair—*The Bridges of Madison County,* to name just one. This theme is not particularly new. Rather, the woman-woman affair is just a new twist on an old story.

In chapter 3 we will look closer at the typical themes and pain that are part of questioning one's gender identity and that propel a woman to adopt a lesbian identity. Nonetheless, women who experience same-sex attraction commonly wonder if they were born gay.[4] They may pose the question, "I never chose the attractions, so why do I have them?" For now, let's turn our attention to the beliefs of our nation concerning the biology of homosexuality and the second question—is anyone born gay?

Born Gay? Genetic Theories: Science or Spin?

In 1993, my husband, John, and I were guests on the Oprah Winfrey show sharing our story of change along with several others who represented an opposing, pro-homosexual view. One of those guests was Dr. Richard A. Isay, a homosexual and professor of psychiatry at Cornell Medical College. During the taping of the show, Dr. Isay loudly reported that soon one of his colleagues would prove without a shadow of a doubt that homosexuality is genetic. And then the commercial break cut off further discussion.

The studio audience immediately accepted Dr. Isay's news, but he never produced this predicted "forthcoming" evidence. His colleague had not discovered a "gay gene" after all. Ten years later, and still no proof has been announced.

With that episode in mind, let's take a look at some of the genetic arguments espoused by the "born gay" apologists. This is scientific information, but it's important to the issues we're discussing. After a quick look at three key studies, we will review some feminist and lesbian opinions about the "born gay" theories.

X-Chromosome Study

No doubt Dr. Isay was referring to the X-chromosome study by prominent gay scientist, Dr. Dean Hamer, published in *Science* on July 16, 1993.[5] In this study, Dr. Hamer and his team claimed to identify a specific region of the X chromosome that two-thirds of gay brothers in families had in common. The news of any correlation between a portion of DNA and homosexual men in families was heralded by the popular press as proof that homosexuality was inherited and innate.

But the methods employed in this study were seriously flawed. Only two years later, the federal Office of Research Integrity investigated Dr. Hamer for research improprieties.

According to Philip L. Bereano, professor of Technology and Public Policy at the University of Washington and national board member of the ACLU,

> Hamer's study is significantly compromised by:
> 1) not checking the straight men in these families

for the *(x-chromosome)* segment; 2) defining who is "gay" by an extreme estimate for the prevalence of homosexuality among American men, 2% (using the commonly accepted estimate of 5-10% eliminates the statistical validity of his results); and 3) knowing that the federal Office of Research Integrity is investigating the study because one of the collaborators has alleged that the research team suppressed data.[6]

Much of the commentary regarding Hamer's study by his fellow geneticists, sociologists, and scientists criticizes the research for employing a small sample size, omitting a control group for comparison, stretching correlation definitions to include additional gay family members (uncles and nephews), as well as a variety of other complicated issues. The most significant criticism of the study is that it has not been replicated—no unrelated laboratory has been able to produce the same findings. Replication establishes some validity or significance to the reported results of the initial study, and without duplication, any finding is called into question.

When researchers in Canada performed the study, the findings were very different, as noted below. The scientific and the gay community alike found fault with the original study's conclusions. Dr. Dean Byrd reported:

> What's more interesting is that when Hamer's study was duplicated by Rice et al.[7] with research that was more robust, the genetic markers were found to be insignificant. Rice concluded, "It is unclear why our results are so discrepant from Hamer's original study. Because our study was larger than that of Hamer's et al., we certainly had adequate power to detect a genetic effect as large as reported in that study. Nonetheless, our data do

not support the presence of a gene of large effect influencing sexual orientation at position XQ28."[8]

The Advocate, the national gay and lesbian newsmagazine, quoted Dr. Hamer in February of 1998 as saying that there is "not a single, all-powerful 'gay gene.'"[9] They also reported Anne Fausto-Sterling, a professor of medical science at Brown University and a lesbian, as saying, "There is not a very good self-critical assessment when people say there is a gene for this or that. If you take a complicated human behavior like shyness, which is modulated over a lifetime, the gap between the behavior and that protein is enormous."

One other observation, though clearly not from an academic perspective, is that of many gays themselves. Consider this recent quote from Peter Tatchell of the gay rights organization Outrage!: "I'm amazed that it's taken this long to destroy what is obviously a totally implausible theory. It is a choice and we should be glad that it's that way and celebrate it for ourselves."[10]

Inner Ear Study

At about the same time that Dr. Hamer himself admitted there was no evidence for a "gay gene," Dennis McFadden, a professor of psychology at the University of Texas, presented a study relating sexual preference in men and women to the inner ear.[11] Dr. McFadden examined 200 adult individuals in four different groups: heterosexual and homosexual women and heterosexual and homosexual men. Some of each group were later identified as bisexual.

What the researchers expected to find was that the cochlea amplifier (specifically used in the process of hearing) would be more sensitive in the women and less so in the men. "Females with their more sensitive cochlea respond more powerfully to this test than do men," said McFadden. "This is true even among infants."[12] "The results," McFadden said, "indicated that lesbians had click-responses that were significantly weaker than those of heterosexual women. The signal was still weaker for all males, both gay and straight." Gay scientist Dr. Michael Bailey of Northwestern University cautiously described the potential cause of the inner ear differences in homosexual women: "The most likely interpretation is that this represents some kind of effect of early hormones on the developing fetus."[13]

Conclusions about this difference were proclaimed by some media sources as proving a biological cause of lesbianism. For example, according to Associated Press science writer Paul Recer, "Researchers say they have found the first strong evidence of a physical difference between lesbians and straight women—a finding that the inner ears of gay women work more like those of men. The discovery adds new support to the *theory* that sexual orientation may be predisposed before birth"[14] (italics mine).

Making his claims more realistic, Dr. McFadden said that androgens may also "alter the brain centers that produce sexual orientation." *"But,"* he said, *"researchers have yet to find a brain structure that determines sexual orientation in women"*[15] (emphasis added). McFadden was also quoted as saying that "Any human behavior is going to be the result of complex intermingling of genetics and environment. It would be astonishing if that were not true for homosexuality."[16]

In fact, McFadden has not proven *why* lesbians' hearing sensitivity varies from heterosexual women. Could it be that exposure to louder sounds in work and social activity might play a role? Or could heterosexual women, as a result of specific interests, train their ears to detect softer sounds—such as through listening to classical music? Were these factors ruled out? Not according to the study abstract.

But the abstract did explain that the subjects studied were warned to avoid intense sounds and various common drugs for the 24 hours before the experiment. This was because Dr.

McFadden knew from his own research published in 1984[17] and 1994[18] that doses of aspirin or quinine produces hearing loss temporarily, particularly the type of hearing that he was analyzing in this study.

But instead of 24 hours of delay after taking aspirin, his own findings in 1984 were that "the recovery process was highly idiosyncratic, with the emissions of some subjects returning to full strength within 24 hours, while for other subjects, full recovery required several days."[19] Dr. McFadden should have waited three or four days after his subjects took aspirin in order to measure hearing because it took that long for all the subjects to recover from the aspirin-related hearing loss.

Has this study *proved* with any amount of certainty that homosexuality is biological? Absolutely not! In fact, McFadden states a possible conclusion:

> Multiple explanations can be generated for the weaker CEOAEs [click-evoked otoacoustic emissions, otherwise described as: echo-like sound waves emitted by normal-hearing cochleas in response to a brief sound stimulus] in homosexual and bisexual females than in heterosexual females. As noted, OAEs [otoacoustic emissions, "sounds that originate in the cochlea and propagate through the middle ear into the external ear canal"[20]] can be diminished by exposures to intense sounds, certain drugs, and other manipulations. *Thus, it may be that something in the lifestyles of homosexual and bisexual females leads them to be exposed to one or more agents that have reduced their CEOAEs, either temporarily or permanently...Under this explanation, the presence of weaker CEOAEs in homosexual and bisexual females is a secondary consequence to the lifestyle adopted by the majority of these women and thus is not conceptually different*

from the hearing loss developed by rock musicians. (italics mine).[21]

Another expert on the subject of the biology of homosexuality, Dr. Jeffrey Satinover, has written, "There is no evidence that homosexuality is simply 'genetic'—*and none of the research itself claims there is.* Only the press and certain researchers do, when speaking in sound bites to the public."[22]

I am amazed that Dr. McFadden is making such dramatic leaps in logic without making serious mention in the press of the more logical possibility that the weaker hearing in homosexual and bisexual women may be "a secondary consequence to the lifestyle adopted by the majority of these women and thus is not conceptually different from the hearing loss developed by rock musicians."[23] Heralding unproven dynamics in the womb as the biological basis for homosexuality in women seems quite unscientific and somewhat unethical when more direct and logical explanations are available.

Finger Length Study

A third recent study attempted to correlate lesbianism with a variance in the finger length of the second and fourth digits of women's hands. In 2000, a team of researchers headed by S. Marc Breedlove, professor of psychology at the University of California at Berkeley, went to street fairs in the San Francisco area and surveyed the public on gender, age, sexual orientation, and handedness as well as other factors, and then concluded by taking a portable photocopy of their hands.

The team then measured the length of the fingers and concluded:

> The right-hand 2D:4D [second and fourth digits] ratio of homosexual women was significantly more masculine (that is, smaller) than that of

heterosexual women, and did not differ significantly from heterosexual men. Thus finger length
ratios, like otoacoustic emissions ["sounds that
originate in the cochlea and propagate through the
middle ear into the external ear canal"[24]], suggest
that at least some homosexual women were
exposed to greater levels of fetal androgen [male
hormone] than heterosexual women."[25]

I find it interesting that Breedlove took the most distant
and unproven possible conclusion from the McFadden experiment to strongly suggest that fetal androgen affected both
finger length and sexual orientation.

We have already discussed the McFadden inner-ear study,
so now let's look at the assertions solely of the Breedlove
finger-length study. Dr. Breedlove built his theory on many
presuppositions: male hormones are present in the mother's
womb apart from a male fetus, "events before birth (or even
before conception in the case of older brothers) influence
sexual orientation," and "men with more elder brothers,
including those men who develop a homosexual orientation,
might be exposed to greater than normal levels of prenatal
androgen" [male hormone].[26] In other words, he states that
homosexual men may be exposed to greater amounts of male
hormone in the womb. In essence, Breedlove and team
attribute the cause of homosexuality in males and females to
the excessive presence of male hormone during fetal development.

Dr. Breedlove makes vast and inconclusive assertions from
the basis of finger length of both males and females.
Although much of the science related to males in this study
is refutable, let's examine a bit more closely the conclusions
related to homosexual and heterosexual females. First of all,
these conclusions are based on "animal models" demon-
strating in Dr. Breedlove's own previous research that extraor-
dinarily high doses of prenatal male hormone in rats, mice,

and hamsters impact the development of the nervous system and brain.[27] Specifically, exceptional doses of steroids impacted the area of the rats' brains responsible for spatial learning and muscular development.[28]

We already know that taking steroids as adults impacts muscular development in both women and men. But Dr. Breedlove's assumptions about the other results in humans have not been verified. In fact, J. Richard Udry, professor of maternal and child health and sociology at University of North Carolina, Chapel Hill, states, "A female fetus produces practically no testosterone herself." By contrast Udry explains,

> This is where the whole thing begins to fall apart. The male fetus produces so much testosterone during the time when gender differences like finger length are taking place, that the amount the mother contributes is trivial. So the idea that androgens from the mother could have a measurable effect on finger length is unlikely.[29]

What exactly did Breedlove's researchers find? If anything, they found a minimal relationship between finger length of two digits on the right hand and homosexuality in women. That relationship, though very weak, shows some form of a correlation. I will let Laurie Essig, a lesbian writer from Salon.com, comment on this aspect:

> This sort of study uses the existence of a statistical correlation to argue causation. Certain sorts of hands may be more likely to appear on the bodies of women who identify as lesbians, but isn't that a correlation as opposed to a cause? People with green eyes might be more likely to be accountants, but it is highly unlikely that there is a causal relationship between the two.[30]

So What Does Science Say After All?

At the moment, science has very little to say about a biological or genetic cause for homosexuality. Most of the research asserting a biological cause has been performed by gay men who were specifically looking for a biological cause.

Even lesbian writers have commented that biological arguments are not conclusive:

> Despite widespread popular appeal and an enthusiastic acceptance among a large subset of gay men, biologically determinist theories have not, by and large, appealed greatly to women who feel under pressure to explain their own erotic inclinations.[31]

Jan Clausen, feminist writer and former lesbian activist, also commented:

> I think it's fine to be straight or gay by choice. What's not okay is to lie about the complex attractions that often culminate in simple labels.... What's got to stop is the rigging of history to make the either/or look permanent and universal. I understand why this argument may seem dangerous to erotic outsiders for whom the public assertion of a coherent, unchanging lesbian or gay identity has proved an indispensable tactic in the battle against homophobic persecution.[32]

Lesbian Psychologies, a volume produced by feminist and lesbian therapists and writers of the Boston Lesbian Psychologies Collective, acknowledges a variety of reasons for adopting a lesbian identity: "Some of us *choose* to be lesbians because we found that in our relationships with women the spiritual qualities and psychological or emotional connections give us great satisfaction and empower us in our own potentials. Some of us *choose* to be lesbians for more strictly political reasons, in order to counter heterosexual privilege and to develop nonaggressive and nonhierarchical structures for interpersonal relationships....Others *feel* we were born lesbians"[33] (italics added for emphasis).

I find it interesting that the public message from the gay community to the outside world is almost uniformly "we were born gay and cannot change. Homosexuality is a gift from God." Yet the messages within the scholarly lesbian community are contradictory. The message by the Boston Lesbian Psychologies Collective was *not* that science insists that people who have same-sex attractions were born that way. Rather it says, "*Others feel...*" And they add this to the mix: "For some of us, the choice to live a lesbian lifestyle is an explicit choice not to live the lives of our parents, and more particularly the lives of our mothers."[34]

Why Are the "Born Gay" Theories So Persuasive?

If the studies are not conclusive and the lesbian community is not necessarily in agreement, why are these arguments so persuasive? I believe that the "born gay" theories are appealing for a couple of reasons. First, they provide an explanation for the feelings of attraction that most women cannot otherwise explain. Perhaps such ideas help a woman understand why she felt "different" or "out of place" among her peers when growing up. In other words, it gives form to her feelings. A person involved in homosexuality might then say, "Ah...I'm gay—that's why other kids treated me poorly when I was growing up."

Second, if a woman or man is "born gay," the inner and outer protest is seemingly silenced. Suddenly, homosexuality could not possibly be a moral issue; it is no longer "wrong." Instead, "homosexuality occurs naturally and is a common variant among humans."[35] How could God condemn someone for being the way she was created? But the Bible, in fact, calls us men and women, not heterosexuals and homosexuals. In reality, the Scriptures refer to homosexuality as a behavior, not as an identity.

Joe Dallas, author and former President of Exodus International, writes,

> Even if homosexuality is someday proven to be inborn, *inborn* does not necessarily mean *normal*.... Second, inborn tendencies toward certain behaviors (such as homosexuality) do not make those behaviors moral. Obesity and violent behavior are now thought to be genetically influenced....Surely we are not going to say that obesity, violence, alcoholism, and adultery are legitimate because they were inherited. So it is with homosexuality. Whether inborn or acquired, it is still, like all sexual contact apart from marriage, immoral. And immoral behavior cannot be legitimized by a quick baptism in the gene pool.[36]

Dr. Hamer makes this statement about the limitations of science: "Biology is amoral; it offers no help in distinguishing between right and wrong. Only people, guided by their values and beliefs, can decide what is moral and what is not."[37]

But if science doesn't adequately explain the causation of homosexuality, what does? In chapter 3 we'll take a closer look at personal experiences matched with over a hundred years of psychological theory and data. Perhaps we may more adequately answer the question of the female struggler: If I am not born gay, where did these feelings come from?

3

Classic Development of Lesbian Attraction

While teaching at the local public high school, I met Natalie, an attractive young student with large brown eyes and brown hair. She was drawn to me, constantly complimenting me on my makeup, eating her lunch near the staff lunchroom, and preferring my company over that of her peers.

My conversations with Natalie had started because of a paper I was writing for a student teaching class at the university. I was supposed to interview a couple of students about their interests and what they wanted to pursue as a career. I had asked Natalie if she would be one of my interviewees, and she had agreed.

Little did I know that this young woman was starving for attention from women whom she respected. As a result, our interview became a bit more complicated than I had anticipated.

During the first part of the interview, I asked my questions and received the answers I needed. Then strangely, the conversation veered off topic as Natalie complimented my makeup.

"I like how you put on your blush," Natalie said. "It always looks attractive and natural—not at all like my mom's. She puts hers on too heavily—probably because my stepfather likes it that way," she added with disgust.

It didn't take a rocket scientist to realize that Natalie had some strong negative feelings toward her mother.

I decided to probe just a bit. "What's your mother like?" I asked.

"She's kind of weak and does whatever my stepfather says," Natalie answered. "They broke up a couple years ago, and I was so glad. My mom had been pushed around enough. He never treated her well—but now he's come back."

Natalie then told me her biological father died when she was four. "Mom had to pay the bills without him, so when she met my stepdad, Joe, she married him," she said sadly. "My stepdad is a real jerk. He's always looking for ways to insult my mom and me. And he was supposed to help us with paying the bills, but he can't keep a job...or doesn't want to. As a result, he's living off of us."

The openness with which Natalie shared with me should have been a clue about her emotional neediness...but I didn't see it then.

Soon, Natalie was walking alongside me whenever I left the classroom, was the first pupil to answer my questions, and smiled profusely whenever I spoke to her for even a minute. Eventually, I noticed her crush-like behavior toward me and decided I needed to gently set a boundary with her.

I'm sure she was a bit hurt at first. But as a teacher, my responsibility was for the emotional, scholastic, and social welfare of the teens, and I knew that what I had done was for her best. In fact, she just needed a bit of prodding to go back and relate with her peers regularly again. And now she knew that I was a "safe" person if she needed to talk.

Some Observations

Although Natalie didn't identify herself as someone who experienced same-sex attraction or had lesbian relationships at that time, I can look back at our conversations and see some strong factors that might propel her into a lesbian relationship at some point. These very dynamics have been present in many other women's lives who have ended up dealing with same-sex attraction.

One major indicator was how Natalie judged her mother's representation of life as a woman, wife, and mother. Her stepfather's poor example of how a man should relate to his wife was also important, as was her struggle to find a female role model whom she could respect.

I've heard this same pattern repeated so often that I felt prompted to ask in the survey I conducted among ex-lesbian women: "Did you want to be like your mother when you were growing up?" More than eight out of ten of the women responded with a resounding, "No!"[1]

When asked, "Which gender seemed to have the more desirable characteristics to be like?" three-quarters of the 265 women responded that men were more desirable role models. When asked their reasons, many of the women answered along this line: "Men are strong and in control, not easily pushed around," or "They are less likely to be victimized."

Each write-in answer that described a positive view of the male role model reflected a negative view of the female. For example, a common positive comment, "Males are respected and valued" implies that females, by contrast, are not "respected or valued."

One woman's response was typical of many others: "I didn't want to be viewed as a sex object, property, weak, or inferior."

Somehow this woman received some powerful messages from her childhood about women. That message may have been that a man sees a woman as a sex object, rather than a valued partner and sexually appealing in a positive sense.

By saying, "I didn't want to be viewed as a sex object, property, weak, or inferior," this particular respondent revealed a climate of misogyny in her home. *Misogyny* is commonly defined as "a hatred of women,"[2] but I would personally describe misogyny as "hatred of the *feminine*," exhibited by actions and words of antagonism toward women, usually starting with women closest to the individual and moving outward. Both men and women can be misogynists. In fact, a woman who internalizes the subtle or not-so-subtle messages from someone in her life who is misogynistic may end up hating women herself. Worse yet, she may become alienated from the feminine in herself.

For this reason, homosexuality can be called a reparative drive—an attempt to repair the missing connection with our own gender, an attempt to love ourselves. Dr. Elizabeth Moberly identified this drive in her ground-breaking book, *Homosexuality: A New Christian Ethic*. Although her investigation centered on male homosexuals, much that she learned can also be applied to females.[3]

A similar view is expressed by Jan Clausen, a former lesbian activist and feminist author (*Apples & Oranges: My Journey to Sexual Identity*). This was her view of female: "I viewed lesbians as a guerrilla insurgency against the gender status quo, so much happier in our beleaguered camaraderie than the huddled masses of concubines and housewives who hugged the safer side of the erotic either/or."[4] Stated another way, she viewed heterosexual women as lesser than homosexual women. Heterosexual married women were seen as "huddled masses" of unthinking "concubines"—sexual slaves.

As she set about writing her story, Clausen explains: "I did not particularly want to remember where I'd come from, to recall the humiliation I associated with conventional femininity, or to revisit the frank contempt in which I'd once held womankind."[5]

With thoughtful reflection and significant self-awareness, Clausen writes: "Throughout my life, questions about desire and struggles with its consequences have connected to my sense of my own gender as a problem. The conviction that being a girl doomed me to a second-rate existence emerged very strongly at a point in my teens..."

Ms. Clausen had some rather strong feelings about the "doom" of being a girl, and yet she was one. Somehow, somewhere, this conflict had to be resolved. Her intellectual connection with boys versus girls in her teenage years may have made boys more attractive to identify with as a peer group. "Why, when I emerged from my childhood garden of solitude, did I turn to a boy for the connection I craved?...It was about what sort of beings seemed to have the gorgeous minds, about who were the movers and shakers.... I'd never met a girl I considered really smart."[6]

Whatever Clausen's reason for her disdain for her own gender, she needed some way to reconcile the two pieces of herself that were at odds. As she entered the lesbian phase of her life, several of her journal entries reveal what she hoped to gain: "Homosexual love is the great rejoicing of finding something that seemed lost ..." She describes her attraction to specific women in her adult life: "She is everything I desire. She is myself—or rather, I am herself."[7] "I'd fallen madly for a gender. All my life I'd had problems with People in Groups. Now I wanted to belong."[8] In place of her designed distance and disdain, Clausen began to embrace a particular form of womanhood. A huge step had taken place toward seeing other women's femaleness as being desirable. For the first time, she wanted to belong to a group of women.

One particular relationship with another woman changed Clausen's concepts about women, giving her some degree of resolution. Somehow as I read her story, I knew she would afterward be free to appreciate her own femaleness and perhaps not be driven to homosexual relationships any longer. "With her, I experimented with a new relation to the 'femininity' I'd been at war with since my teens.... If femme could be a role and not a fate—then maybe it needn't demolish my self-respect to make love to a man I desired."[9]

Clausen later talks about leaving her lesbian lover of 12 years, as well as the entire lesbian life and culture, for a man with whom she fell in love on a trip to Nicaragua. "I couldn't bear the dividedness any longer....I left [lesbian life], in the end, because I couldn't bear confinement. I left because my future was dying and I had to rescue it... I left because I needed a life of my own."[10]

Almost by chance, Clausen was able to reunite with the feminine side of herself—to love herself without projecting that need onto other women. And from there she was able to move on in her emotional connection and respect for her own womanhood. Perhaps it's a rarity to move on to more complete internal feminine identification while in lesbian life and relationships, but her experience clearly illustrates that lesbian attraction is an attempt to love and be reunited with the female part of oneself.

Latasha's Story

Let's look at another angle in the development of lesbian attraction. Latasha grew up in a social atmosphere where women were looked at as sexual objects and subjected to sexual abuse. The story of her life squarely fits the definition of a misogynistic (hatred of women or the feminine) environment created by the men in her life.

Latasha's family lived in southern Florida. Her mother was chronically depressed, even before Latasha was born, and abused both verbally and emotionally by her possessive and angry husband. His rage was all the more directed sexually at his wife after he had been drinking.

Latasha's mom was very involved with the choir at their local church, but her faith never really impacted her home life. Her mother seemed so weak, unable to stand up to her dad. Once, when Latasha was in fourth or fifth grade, she witnessed her father raping her mother after a drinking bout. "I was so *angry!*" Latasha exclaimed. "I should have been able to help her, to stop it!

"That was when I decided I wanted to be a boy," she recounted. "I became a tomboy and acted and fought like a boy. Instead of trying on my mom's makeup and playing with dolls, I opted for climbing trees, wrestling, and riding bikes. At about this same time I began to develop crushes on some of my female teachers."

Latasha told me that her room at home was a refuge— "neutral territory." As a result her mother often retreated there to avoid the havoc raging in the other parts of the house. Her mom found safety in Latasha's presence. In a very subtle way, Latasha was getting the unspoken message from her mom that she was her mom's protector.

Latasha's much older brothers were womanizers with stacks of pornography in their rooms, where they often had promiscuous sex with girls. Eventually Latasha discovered that both of her parents had been having extra-marital affairs. Her break from her family's form of heterosexuality was a desperate attempt to survive emotionally. She later told me,

> I felt that I could treat a woman better than a man could—the way a woman should have been treated. I didn't want to identify with the "weaker species," but I wanted to take care of them. I was certain I was born gay because I wanted to be a boy and felt different from the other girls.
>
> In junior high school, as the other girls were blooming and changing, my hormones led me toward crushes on girls. But by high school, I had

entered what I now call my 'bisexual stage.' I call it that because although I was attracted to girls, I was trying to fit in and I found that I could be attracted to boys physically. Yet following the brief physical attraction, I would be done with them. Girls, on the other hand, made me stutter, get nervous, and wonder to myself, *What am I going to say and do?* Sometimes straight girls would flirt with me, and I found that really exciting and flirted back. They were just playing with me, but I took it very seriously. But it wasn't until college that I decided that men were a waste of my time. *I am gay,* I declared to myself, and I set about looking for a wife, my modified version of the American dream. I don't know what I would have done without being able to define myself as gay. I put my hope in being gay—I would not be destined to duplicate my family's pattern of life.

Let's look a bit more closely at the individual factors that drove Latasha to crave female affection sexually.

Childhood Trauma

Both Chris (from chapter 1) and Latasha witnessed forms of abuse against their mothers. As a result, both made vows not to be like their mothers—weak and vulnerable. Each of the women patterned themselves after males, rejecting their own female qualities and becoming predominately involved in male activities. Thus the adopted term—tomboys.

According to the survey I conducted of former lesbians, more than 60 percent witnessed some form of abuse against a family member. An astounding 90 percent experienced some form of abuse themselves.[11]

The three most common forms of abuse experienced before the age of 18 by these women were emotional (almost

70 percent), sexual (more than 60 percent), and verbal abuse (more than half of the women).

Of those sexually abused by men, the majority (almost 70 percent) were molested by a male that did not fit in the "family" or "friends" categories. The next two largest groups of offenders were "family friend" and "other male family member," which did not include father, stepfather, brother, or stepbrother. Both of these categories accounted for one quarter of the incidents, but brothers were not far behind at 20 percent of the reported molesters.

The incidence of sexual abuse among lesbians is incredibly high when compared to national estimates of sexual abuse against women in general. Commonly used statistics claim that 25[12] or 17[13] percent of the women in the United States will be sexually assaulted at some point during their lifetimes. But more than 60 percent of the women surveyed experienced *childhood* sexual abuse! My statistics do not even include sexual assault after the age of 18. According to Dr. Stanton Jones, "Experience of sexual abuse as a child, in other words, more than tripled the likelihood of later reporting homosexual orientation."[14]

According to the Third National Incidence Study of Child Abuse and Neglect (NIS-3),[15] the most extensive research that has been done in the U.S. on child abuse and neglect, the occurrence of these sins against children is on the rise. These are the four major findings:

- Girls were sexually abused three times more often than boys.

- Boys had a greater risk of emotional neglect and serious injury than did girls.

- Children are consistently vulnerable to sexual abuse from age three on.

■ The incidence of maltreatment did not vary according to race.[16]

The impact of childhood trauma and abuse on the adult woman can be absolutely devastating. Abuse writes on the heart and soul of the female child what seem to be indelible messages about her sense of self, her relationships, and her ability to trust others.

Dr. Nancy Faulkner reviewed clinical findings on childhood sexual abuse in her article, "Pandora's Box: The Secrecy of Child Sexual Abuse." Dr. Faulkner wrote, "Victims of sexual abuse frequently experience feelings of shame, guilt, isolation, powerlessness, embarrassment, and inadequacy. They may even accept responsibility for the abuse by blaming themselves."[17]

Rosie O'Donnell wrote in her recent book, *Find Me,* in which she identified herself as a lesbian,

> I was an abused kid. This is something I have chosen not to dwell on in my public life....So, yes, I had been abused, although the details are not important. What is important is that I had, supposedly, dealt with the fallout in therapy. How naïve I was. Abuse is an ongoing saga for everyone who has lived through it. It may start and stop in real time, but in mind-time it goes on forever.

O'Donnell then shares an example of her ongoing saga. "Why was I drawn to Stacie?" [Stacie is a young woman she was trying to help escape an abusive situation.] "Oh, a million reasons, one of which was this: a reliving. A sense of shared pain."[18]

In very vulnerable statements, Rosie describes her motivation for helping others today: "To put it bluntly, I have no boundaries. Zero, nada, zippo—none... I am in constant savior mode. Like it or not, I hear their voices [birth mothers with the adoption agency she supports], I see their faces, I don the tights and cape. Here I come to save the day!...It's a compulsion. I can't help myself."[19] Later in her book, she postulates:

> Maybe it's also an abuse thing. When your boundaries have been violated, you just plain and simple stop *seeing* the space between people, so people's pain becomes your pain and you have to stop it. At the same time, though, codependency is also a distancing ploy; you're so busy trying to save the world out there you forget about the people close to you, and then, last of all, or first of all, you forget about yourself, that you might be the one worth saving.[20]

Another nuance from some of the stories from women in my survey has been the effects of sexual abuse from older females.[21] When this happens, the young girl may wonder if perhaps she is lesbian because she experienced some degree of pleasure—first from the attention an older girl gave her, and second, from the sexual activity itself.

Instead of being more of an aggressive act, these violations tended to be more seductive in nature. One woman shared with me that she had received sexual attention from a female babysitter when she was quite young, around the age of five. This woman was reluctant to admit that the contact had been sexual abuse because it met a need for older female attention that her mother wasn't able to give her. But the experience did cause her to question her sexual identity at a very young age.

So childhood abuse or witnessing abuse can lead a girl to reject her own female self early on.[22] This early rejection is seen clearly in many ways, so we will examine it in the next section. If childhood abuse, trauma, or specifically sexual abuse is something that you or your loved one may have experienced, you can learn more about healing from abuse in chapter 6.

Gender Role Rejection

Gender role rejection is a deliberate, almost constant, and somewhat inflexible adoption of male interests and attributes by a female child. A long-term expert in gender identity disorder (GID), George A. Rekers, Ph.D., has researched a great deal about GID and has published more than 55 articles in professional journals. Dr. Rekers has much to say about psychological sex role development:

> As part of the process of normal gender identity in the family, young children will often try out a variety of sex role behaviors as they learn to make the fine distinctions between masculine and feminine roles. Some young boys occasionally perform behaviors that our culture traditionally has recognized as feminine, such as wearing a dress, using cosmetics or play acting the roles of bearing and nursing infants. Similarly, many young girls will occasionally assume a masculine role—pretending to be "daddy" while playing house, or temporarily adopting a cluster of masculine behaviors which leads to the social designation of "tomboy." This type of temporary and episodic exploration of cross-sex-typed behaviors is typical of many boys and girls and usually constitutes a learning experience in the process of normal sex role socialization (Maccoby & Jacklin, 1974, Mischel, 1970; Serbin, 1980)...In pathological cases [where gender identity disorder exists], however, children deviate from the normal pattern of exploring masculine and feminine behaviors and develop an inflexible, compulsive, persistent and rigidly stereotyped

pattern (Zucker, 1985)....Although little research exists on female childhood gender disorders, it is possible to identify the parallel conditions of maladaptive hyperfemininity and hypermasculinity in girls (Rekers & Mead, 1979, 1980). (For more information about the studies Rekers cites, see his article in *The Journal of Human Sexuality*.)[23]

Marisa's Story

Marisa was another young woman I spoke with about leaving lesbianism. Marisa was a very attractive woman in her twenties with sparkling eyes and a great sense of humor. She described her childhood to me.

> My parents were always fighting [verbally] with each other. I remember early on, playing with dolls and putting on my mom's makeup. But I remember a time when I decided, *forget dolls! I'm going to go climb trees, play ball, and rough-house with the boys.* In elementary school I noticed what other girls were interested in—they all wore dresses, played with dolls, and did their nails. I didn't fit in. Instead, in my play time I got into the father role while playing house.

What Marisa and so many others describe is an "an inflexible, compulsive, persistent and rigidly stereotyped pattern" of masculinized behavior.[24] More than just a tomboy image, I see it as "tomboy with a purpose" of not identifying themselves with their female role model—Mother.

Marisa, Latasha, and Chris are not the only examples of this dynamic. Almost 90 percent of the women in my survey who are in the process of personally overcoming homosexuality identified themselves as tomboys in childhood. In addition, more than 60 percent were mistaken for a boy at some time as a child.

Childhood Play Patterns

Dr. Elaine Siegel was a psychoanalyst to lesbian patients who were not seeking change from homosexuality. She describes her initial views on female homosexuality:

> To be a liberal and liberated woman and yet to view homosexuality as a result of untoward development seemed at times a betrayal of all I then believed. But viewing my patients through the lens of psychoanalytic thinkers and clinicians soon showed me that allowing myself to be seduced into perceiving female homosexuality as a normal lifestyle would have cemented both my patients and myself into a rigid mode that precluded change of whatever nature.[25]

Dr. Siegel studied sex-typed behaviors in childhood doll play and reports, "Doll play is seen by [researcher J. Kestenberg] as the principle outlet. In my group of patients, such games were conspicuously absent (Siegel, 1986). They could not recall ever really playing."[26]

In the foreword to Dr. Siegel's book, Theo Dorpat, M.D. wrote,

> Dr. Siegel found that all her female homosexual patients were uninterested as children in their dolls or in the usual games of childhood. She demonstrates that [they were unable to] establish gender identity via introjection and identification with significant others (chiefly their mothers). Female homosexuality arises from the need of certain women who were traumatized early in their development to repair their defective body images by

seeking others like themselves. The psychoanalytic investigations of Dr. Siegel and other analysts before her show that the lesbian's interest in women is a vicarious way of enjoying other women's femininity. [27]

This observation led Dr. Siegel to her psychoanalytic conclusion:

> A woman whose body is her own, that is, who has successfully integrated her sexual organ and her sexual self within her total inner self representation, is able to meet a potential male partner without either resenting him or competing with his maleness. For the women I treated, this was at first an insurmountable task because they had to acquire a more complete body image and sense of self.[28]

From another point of view, Dr. Stanton Jones, provost of Wheaton College and coauthor of *Modern Psychotherapies*, reviews the evidence of causative factors of homosexuality in his new book, *Homosexuality: The Use of Scientific Research in the Church's Moral Debate.*

> There is general agreement that childhood manifestations of gender nonconformity (such as a boy's interest in girl's company, toys, play, clothing and so on) appear to predispose the boy to adult homosexuality....Researchers recently conducted a large analysis of the research on the relationship between sex-typed behaviors and sexual orientation. They concluded that "for both men and women, research has firmly established that homosexual subjects recall substantially more cross-sex-typed behavior in childhood than do heterosexual subjects."[29] In other words, the best

research to date suggests a relationship between homosexuality in adulthood and gender nonconformity in childhood."[30]

So early childhood behavior, such as an avoidance of typical female games and activities, a preference of male playmates over female ones, and an unwillingness or rejection of typical female interests in a routine or hard and fast way can be significant. These should be seen as indicators of how a girl sees and accepts herself as a female in childhood. Keep in mind, though, that the research that Dr. Rekers has reviewed over many years shows that brief episodes into opposite gender stereotypical play is part of learning how to be a little girl. Also, this alone does not predispose a female to homosexual attraction later in life.

Parent-Child Relationships

Therapist Steven Donaldson explained in a lecture given at the Evergreen Conference in 2002:

> Parents have a tremendous influence on the formation of a child's self-perception....We must understand that children are born in a completely dependent state. They need not only food, shelter, and clothing, but attention, acceptance, approval, and affection. They need these emotional supplies as much as they need food or water. They have no other source for these supplies. They need them from their own parents.[31]

An infant needs to progress through stages to achieve a healthy image of himself or herself. I am going to share with you a version of an early childhood psychosexual development theory that I first became aware of at a lecture given by Steven Donaldson in Portland, Oregon.

Mother-Daughter Relationship

The theory goes like this: In the earliest phase, from birth to two and a half years, the baby girl attaches to her primary caregiver through learning that her mother is trustworthy and reliable. For example, when she needs food or milk, she cannot prepare it for herself, but Mommy can and does. When she needs a diaper change, the baby girl cannot do that for herself either, but Mommy can and does.

Through this process, the baby girl comes to associate closely with her mother. As you might imagine, neglect on the part of the mother or primary caregiver can wreak havoc on this desired outcome. Instead of learning that she's safe and her caregiver is trustworthy, the baby girl may instead get the message that her mother (or other) is not reliable. Therefore, she may decide to not identify with or trust her mother.

That first period of development continues on with another chief objective—to come to a relatively accurate view of herself and the world immediately around her. The end result should be *trust*. Let me give you another example of what I mean. Let's say the baby girl made it through the first hurdle adequately and takes the attachment with her mother for granted, as she should. She doesn't doubt her mother's attention, affection, and attachment.

She then begins becoming her own person, independent of Mom in small but significant ways. Developmentally speaking, toddlers begin to sit up on their own at about six months, crawl back and forth within the few months following, and then walk by about a year. In that process, we venture out into our world (the living or family room) apart from Mom. We each began our voyage of independent action and independent identity early in life, but we also toddled between our newfound abilities and attachment.

Each of my little boys explored their new abilities by walking a few steps under my watchful eye, but at times they fell and hurt themselves. At that point, they needed me to hold and comfort them. Then they were ready to venture out and try again. If they felt threatened or hurt in any way, they would temporarily return to me for comfort and security. I remember my son Alex first learning to walk at about a year old. We were shopping, and the beat of the music in the department store inspired him to take extra steps. Our whole family applauded as he took 12, then 14 steps, and he turned back to see our excitement and approval. I still remember the proud look of achievement on his face. What a precious memory!

But unfortunately, problems can occur that are rooted in the mother's (or primary caregiver's) lack of personal security. Dr. Siegel's work with her lesbian patients describes a particular type of inadequate mother relationship.

> Their mothers were unable to promote their daughters' identification with their own female-ness and femininity. The mothers are described as immature and emotionally fragile persons who held themselves aloof from the needs of their daughters. The mothers did not treat their daughters as whole persons, rather as split-off parts of themselves. There was a reversal of parent and child roles in which the mothers expected to be nurtured by their own daughters.[32]

Toddlers seem driven to conquer physical independence, yet they need the security that their mothers offer. According to Steven Donaldson, the mother's essential tasks related to both her female and male children are "1) to provide unconditional love and security and 2) to encourage the child's autonomy."[33] A major developmental task for the daughter is to create a separate female identity from her mother.

Sounds so simple, doesn't it? What could possibly go wrong? Unfortunately, in some cases the mother resents, resists, or stifles the baby's sense of safe yet independent exploration. These mothers, like those in Dr. Siegel's research, see their children as part of themselves and emotionally regret their daughters' independence.

Dr. Siegel writes:

> Cecilia's mother quite openly used her little girl as the devalued servant part of her own narcissistic self. The child was expected to function as the mother's maid. Tanya's mother did not seem to recognize the infant as a separate entity at all. Delilah clearly was a replacement child...she was expected to provide what had been lost...Each of these women [mothers of her clients] reversed roles with her child, expecting to be nurtured by [the daughter].[34]

Or perhaps the mother isn't emotionally available for her daughter. Emotional abandonment is terrifying to a young child. "Children experience panic at the thought of the loss of or withdrawal of a parent's approval. It is even more intense than the fear of death. It is the experience of losing their existence...as if they had never existed at all. This is referred to as annihilation anxiety."[35]

Dr. Siegel continues her conclusions about the mother-child relationships of her clients: "The daughters recalled in great detail how they had often been emotionally abandoned and how hard they had tried to please their mothers. Of course, they blamed themselves entirely for the failure..."[36]

Father-Daughter Relationships

Meanwhile, a healthy relationship between father and daughter progresses out of the secure nurturing and independence of the mother-daughter relationship. The little girl, secure in her mother's approval, encouragement, and acceptance, toddles into her daddy's arms. The father is meant to reflect back to the daughter her worth as a female through appreciation and adoration.

Unfortunately, some fathers are not safe or emotionally available to encourage this joy of "girlhood" within the daughter. If the father is abusive to his wife, if he is somehow threatened by his daughter's femininity, or if he is abusive toward his daughter, she is less likely to enjoy her femaleness.

A little girl naturally adores and admires her daddy. I remember early on when I felt that special relationship with my dad and was called "Daddy's girl." That name was a badge of honor to me. Somehow over the next few years, instead of continuing in that pattern, something shifted, and I began to pattern myself after my dad in order to regain his attention. For example, I learned to golf, not because I was particularly interested but because I could do that with my dad.

In her comments about the father-daughter dynamics of her patients, Dr. Elaine Siegel concludes,

> Despite [the women's] deep inner yearnings to win the approval of their families and their later attempts to change family dynamics, they could not wring compassion from their fathers....I suspect that the self-images of their fathers were severely assaulted by being confronted with their "imperfect" daughters. Nevertheless, in their workday behavior the daughters behaved with the same zeal, inventiveness, and courage as their fathers.[37]

If the father is hostile, abusive, or emotionally unavailable to his daughter, he communicates a bad feeling about being a woman to the daughter. And here is still another twist: If the mother is jealous of the father-daughter relationship, the daughter can also become very insecure. The daughter wants to know the strength of her parents' love for each other, as well as the confident strength of her mother. This very dynamic, according to psychoanalytic theory, enables the little girl to wish to be like her mother and desire marriage.

Personality Temperament

Dr. Siegel described her patients in childhood as "talented and quite precocious.[38] I have noticed the aptitude of women I have interviewed over many years, especially in their ability to pick up the unspoken messages in their families. Davies and Rentzel, in their book *Coming Out of Homosexuality*, write,

> Inborn temperament and body build affect girls' early development too. Often people expect a young daughter to be soft, sweet, and compliant, but some come out of the womb hollering, kicking, and looking like they are ready to train for the triathlon. If the girl's parents are also aggressive and athletic, or at least enjoy these characteristics, she probably will grow into a strong, confident heterosexual woman. But sometimes a mother will struggle to accept an aggressive, active daughter, and the little girl will sense her mother's ambivalence. Feeling wounded and rejected, the girl may further detach from her mother, cutting herself off from the source of love she needs to help her grow into her own female identity. In turn, she is left with a same-sex love deficit, leaving her vulnerable to future lesbian involvement.[39]

What Causes Female Same-Sex Attraction?

As we've seen, many influences are implicated in the development of same-sex attraction: childhood trauma, including incidents of sexual abuse, gender role rejection, atypical childhood play patterns, damaged mother-daughter relationships, unhealthy father-daughter relationships, and personality temperament. Researchers from practically all viewpoints agree that a strong combination of factors probably propel a man or woman toward same-sex attraction.

Biological factors may be found to contribute to homosexual feelings in adulthood, but science has produced no evidence of this. Perhaps surprisingly, the Bible has a stronger comment to say about our nature—referring to our natural *sinful* nature. "Surely I was sinful at birth, sinful from the time my mother conceived me," King David exclaims. "Surely you desire truth in the inner parts; you teach me wisdom in the inmost place. Cleanse me with hyssop, and I will be clean; wash me, and I will be whiter than snow" (Psalm 51:5-7). And regarding the nature of man and woman to go astray from God's design, the Bible teaches us, "We all, like sheep, have gone astray, each of us has turned to his own way; and the LORD has laid on him the iniquity of us all" (Isaiah 53:6).

According to the Bible, each of us is born with a disposition of heart and action against our Designer, but He has made up for our inborn deficit, our bent toward sin (defined as missing God's mark). He sacrificed his only Son, Jesus Christ, as payment of our debt, and He promises us a new nature, one that is not in opposition to His will. The apostle Paul writes in his letter to the Roman Christians:

> Those who live according to the sinful nature have their minds set on what that nature desires; but those who live in accordance with the Spirit have their minds set on what the Spirit desires. The mind of sinful man is death, but the mind controlled by the Spirit is life and peace; the sinful mind is hostile to God. It does not submit to God's law, nor can it do so. Those controlled by the sinful nature cannot please God (Romans 8:5-8).

Paul goes on to explain much of the relationship between our old nature, our new nature, and our obedience in an incredible way throughout the book of Romans, but I will conclude with this: Scripturally speaking, we were predisposed to have a sinful nature, not necessarily a homosexual one. But the benefits of being "born again" into God's heavenly family include forgiveness of our sins through Jesus, a new nature that desires to obey God's laws, and an eternal inheritance that cannot be taken away.

This must be why Paul exclaimed: *"Therefore, if anyone is in Christ, he is a new creation; the old has gone, the new has come!"* (2 Corinthians 5:17) and *"I consider that our present sufferings are not worth comparing with the glory that will be revealed in us"* (Romans 8:18).

4

Healthy Female Gender Development

I still laugh when I remember little Karlyn coming to play at our house after church. Timmy, my oldest son, was four years old and preferred playing with boys, but Karlyn was the exception. Somehow they decided that Timmy could play the superhero role and her Beanie Babies would need his protection. The arrangement was very cute from a mom's point of view.

> *God saw all that He had made, and it was very good (Genesis 1:31).*

Karlyn had come to our house still in her church clothes—a beautiful lace dress, a cutesy bow in her curled hair, snow white tights, and polished dress shoes. I gently suggested she change into something more comfortable so she wouldn't get her nice dress dirty. But since John and I have boys, we didn't have little girl clothes. I picked out the most non-masculine colors I could from the closet and said, "Here are your choices, Miss Karlyn. Which would you like to wear?"

The look of disgust on Karlyn's face just about reduced me to laughter.

"No, thank you," she said politely as she turned to run off and play.

"Karlyn, we can't have you running around in your nice clothes, and we don't have any cute little girl clothes at our house, so let's look again. Perhaps we can find something else," I encouraged.

Reluctantly, she followed me again, made the same face, but picked out something that would do. I could almost read her thoughts. *Well, I guess I can do this for an hour.* And then off she went with her Beanie Babies.

I might have considered Karlyn a tomboy simply because she was so active and didn't balk at playing with boys, but she drew some obvious lines limiting how far she would go in identifying with them. Clothing was clearly one of those lines! I had to admire her attitude.

Evidence of Healthy Female Identity

When she's not playing with Timmy, Karlyn prefers to play with Bitty Baby or Hello Kitty toys. Many times I have seen her nurture her little dolls, brush their hair, feed them, or take them shopping. If we had purchased a Batman toy and given it to her for her fourth birthday, she would have said thank you politely under the corrective eye of her mother, but Hello Kitty toys really light up her whole face. Thankfully, Karlyn is very much identifying with her mother and enjoying being a girl.

In contrast to the experiences of the women I described in the previous chapter who sustained much damage in early childhood, being a little girl is meant to be fun, imaginative, and engaging. Instead of completely rejecting doll play, little girls given fertile ground to grow in are commonly interested in playing "mommy" and nurturing their dollies. They identify themselves as female characters in play, such as Cinderella, Pocahontas, Ariel, Batgirl, and others.

They don't all love the same things, but they draw healthy distinctions between girls and boys.

Julie, a neighbor and friend of mine, described herself as a "tomboy" growing up. She told me about taking her oldest daughter, Hannah, to the shoe store to pick out her own shoes for the first time. Julie was hoping that Hannah, who was then three, would pick out the practical ones for everyday play. In fact, Julie kept directing her daughter back to the "less frivolous shoes."

"No, Mommy," Hannah insisted, "I like the ones with the sparkles." Hannah would *not* be dissuaded. She just had to have the sparkly shoes! Hannah is now eight years old and still loves the really girly things: sparkles in her lip gloss, bows, frilly clothes, and such. She is also great at soccer and can play well with boys but prefers to play with other girls. Although her little brother's friends (Timmy, for example) are not very exciting to her, she will play with them—but only if no one else is available!

A grown woman communicates her secure feminine identity when her inward contentment and security radiate to others through her face and eyes. We display our emotions, attitudes, and perspective nonverbally—probably more than we think. This is especially evident when a woman encounters personal tragedy. The world watches and marvels when a woman expresses faith and confidence in God amid adversity and grief.

Lisa Beamer is a wonderful example of a godly woman who responded with grace and trust in God in such a time. Her husband, Todd Beamer, and a group of other men on board United Airlines Flight 93 attempted to recover control of the aircraft from terrorists on that infamous day of September 11, 2001.

Through the use of cell phones on the flight, several of the passengers had heard about the earlier tragic events of that day—that terrorists had hijacked two other planes and deliberately crashed them into the twin towers of New York City's World Trade Center. Upon hearing such news, several men decided to try to overpower the hijackers of their flight. Todd was heard in the background of a cell phone call saying, "Let's roll."

Todd Beamer and the group of men aboard the aircraft were unsuccessful at gaining control of the cockpit. But because of their heroic actions, the plane crashed into a Pennsylvania field instead of exploding into the White House or the Capitol Building. Todd, the crew of the aircraft, and all of the other passengers perished in their brave attempt to wrestle control from violent men.

Lisa, a mother of two and pregnant with their third child, responded with faith and confidence even as she grappled with the loss of her husband. Just three months after September 11, Lisa accepted an invitation to be on Larry King Live on Christmas Eve, 2001. When asked by Mr. King if the tragedy that took her husband's life had caused her to question her faith as a Christian, she responded boldly and with grace.

"It didn't," she replied seriously. "[Dealing with my father's death when I was fifteen] led me to a place where I understand that just because I have faith in God doesn't mean that He is going to prevent every horrible thing from happening to me...or take me away from the difficulties that this world brings to us. But that He is going to screen those difficulties and only allow those in that He wants to allow in. And then, through the difficulties, [He will] certainly continue to show His love for me and the promise that I'm going to spend eternity with Him in heaven. That is the perspective that I was able to get after a few years of grappling with my father's death and the perspective that came to me on September 11 and has stuck like glue since then."[1]

The apostle Peter commends specific characteristics of married women in 1 Peter 3. "Your beauty...should be that of your inner self, the unfading beauty of a gentle and quiet spirit, which is of great worth in God's sight. For this is the way the holy women of the past who put their hope in God used to make themselves beautiful....You are [Sarah's] daughters if you do what is right and do not give way to fear" (1 Peter 3:3-6). Lisa Beamer was a beautiful modern-day woman who fully trusted God in the face of tragedy.

But how do women become Lisa Beamers? Or better yet—how does any woman become the woman she was designed to be by God? How can she overcome all her insecurities and become a woman of confidence in all she does and is—a woman who celebrates her gift of femaleness?

Those of us who have found freedom from our same-sex attractions through faith in Jesus Christ take our understanding of God's purpose for humankind (and women in particular) from the Bible. And the very first book of the Bible—Genesis—tells us a great deal about that purpose.

The Order of Creation

The Bible tells us in its opening passages, "In the beginning God created the heavens and the earth" (Genesis 1:1). It then gives an account of the order in which He created the world and its inhabitants. Repeated throughout the account of the first five days of creation are the words, "And God saw that it was good" (Genesis 1:10). Again and again that phrase records God's delight in His creation.

But after the sixth day, we read, "God saw all that he had made, and it was *very* good" (Genesis 1:31). This positive declaration is made after the formation of man and woman.

On this sixth day, God created a new creature in His own likeness that would inhabit the earth. God defined male and female creations as both existing in His image. In other words, male and female together represent the image of God, and that remains true even today in our fallen world that has strayed so far from God's original design.

When a more in-depth account of day six is given in the second chapter of Genesis, we see the initial creation of the first man, Adam. Soon after, God gives Adam his first lesson.

> The LORD God formed the man from the dust of the ground and breathed into his nostrils the breath of life, and the man became a living being....The LORD God took the man and put him in the Garden of Eden to work it and take care of it....The LORD God said, "It is not good for the man to be alone. I will make a helper suitable for him (Genesis 2:7,15,18).

In verse 18 we read that man by himself was incomplete...alone. I find it interesting that Adam was aware of his need and that aloneness before God provided the solution. We continue the story in Genesis 2:21-25:

> So the LORD God caused the man to fall into a deep sleep; and while he was sleeping, he took one of the man's ribs and closed up the place with flesh. Then the LORD God made a woman from the rib he had taken out of the man, and he brought her to the man. The man said, "This is now bone of my bones and flesh of my flesh; she shall be called 'woman,' for she was taken out of man." For this reason a man will leave his father and mother and be united to his wife, and they will become one flesh. The man and his wife were both naked, and they felt no shame (Genesis 2:21-25).

What an incredibly beautiful account of the creation of man—male and female. How vast is God's wisdom and knowledge! He made man from the earth, but woman from man. Many have noted when reviewing this portion of Scripture that God made woman not from man's heel but from his side. Not to be used and abused but to be loved as a partner and companion.

God wanted to give Adam not an inferior helper but a suitable one. In all of the creation at that time, no suitable helper had been found for Adam, and he had felt his aloneness. Now he immediately accepted Eve and received her as his wife, his partner.

When I read this portion of Scripture as a young Christian, I misconstrued the meaning and richness of the creation. Instead of showing the worth and value of woman alongside that of man, I believed that God had made woman as an afterthought. In fact, I felt as if He had almost forgotten to make her. Because of my own experiences, I couldn't understand that the woman had *not* been an afterthought but was created in a very deliberate manner for a specific purpose. Had God not said, "In the image of God he created him; male and female he created them"? (Genesis 1:27). God defined man as one unit comprised of both the male and the female.

Many years later I finally understood the meaning of this passage and found great delight in it. Notice again that man was made from the earth, but woman was made from man. Why is that important? Women, by our God-given nature, are naturally designed to connect with others. Our sexual bent is also very relational. God created us with the drive to help and support others from a position of strength, not neediness. I suspect this is why heterosexual women often need emotional closeness with their husbands in order to be able to enjoy sexual intimacy.

We must keep in mind that very soon after the account of creation, woman and man are deceived into disobeying God, and from then on mankind has been marred by sin and the sinful nature. From that point forward, no one but the Christ Himself is born with a perfect nature that is not in opposition to our Creator God.

The rest of the Bible is the account of man's (as both male and female) generations of error and deliberate rebellion against our divine Creator, our failure to love and obey Him, and God's divine plan to bring His creation back into whole relationship with Him. John Eldredge and Brent Curtis entitled their book about this intimacy, *The Sacred Romance*. What a fitting title!

Now that we have some idea of God's original design for woman and His delight in His creation—us—let's consider the development of healthy gender identity in girls.

Mothers

A firm foundation for a little girl's security as a female is constructed in many stages. Numerous challenges to this foundation await every girl along the path to womanhood. But as we understand those challenges, we can help our children overcome them, and we can look back on our own wounded childhood and help ourselves heal from their effects.

The first important building block for a secure female child is a mother who enjoys being a woman and cherishes her role as a wife and mother. A girl who observes her satisfied mother will receive the important message that being a girl is a good thing. Such a confident woman is described in the Bible this way: "A wife of noble character who can find? She is worth far more than rubies....She is clothed with strength and dignity; she can laugh at days to come" (Proverbs 31:10, 25).

A second building block is a mother who loves her husband and seeks to support his goals—and his role as a male. Instead of communicating that she is a helpless victim of circumstances or of her possibly abusive husband, she accepts her responsibility in building a trusting relationship with her husband. "Her husband has full confidence in her and lacks nothing of value. She brings him good, not harm, all the days of her life" (Proverbs 31:11-12). She participates in building a climate of trust and security within the home, providing good soil for her marriage and children to grow in.

A third important building block is a father (or father figure) who does not degrade his wife but instead cherishes her and expresses his love for her. Here's an example from Proverbs 31: "Her children arise and call her blessed. Her husband also, and he praises her, 'Many women do noble things, but you surpass them all.' "

Fathers have a special role in reinforcing the truth that a woman is worthy of trust and respect. This attitude spills down from the husband-wife relationship and impacts a couple's children. The male children of such a committed couple learn how to treat girls appropriately, and girls learn that being a woman is worthwhile and desirable.

The natural result of this environment is that a little girl grows up realizing that her mother is strong and capable and that being a woman is good. She will naturally desire to be like her mother. As she imitates her mother and her mother or father praises or acknowledges these attempts, she will most likely conclude that she can succeed in the role of female.

Let me give you a real-life example of a couple I know from my church. Todd and Jennifer married young and began having children right away—two daughters in succession and then a son. Jennifer is very talented at many things—particularly singing, but also at organizing others, graphic layout, sewing, and cooking, to name just a few. She is confident and secure as a mother and has been emotionally present for her young children, all the while using her natural gifts, including singing on the praise teams at our church.

Todd was steady, reliable, and emotionally in touch with his wife and kids as they grew. He admits it hasn't always been easy—every family has challenges—but he has worked hard to maintain warm and affectionate relationships with his wife and children. Their middle child, Alexis, once told me, "When Mom would get stressed because of our budget, Dad would even things out a bit [emotionally] and say, 'Don't worry, I will take care of it.' Dad took the protective, responsible role, and that enabled everyone to kind of relax."

Alexis, now 19, shared with me her view of her mother when she was young. "I really looked up to my mom in a lot of ways, wanting to be like her. In third grade, my girlfriend and I started a band and performed one of my mom's songs in the talent show at school. I did that because my mom had been in bands and I wanted to be just like her. It was terrible, though—we just were not talented in the same way!"

I enjoyed Todd's description of his daughters. "Both of my girls are very athletic but gorgeous. They were both homecoming queens. Todd's voice swelled with pride as he spoke with me. It was obvious to me that he showered his daughters with words of adoration and encouragement.

When I mentioned his comments to Alexis, she told me, "Daddy always has a ready comment to encourage me, and that gives me such motivation in my life. I am a really lucky girl!"

Healthy, Not Perfect Parenting

Alexis and her sister have received a good foundation on which to build a secure feminine identity. That doesn't mean her parents were perfect, but they set a positive example for their children. None of us is a perfect parent here on earth, and when we make mistakes, we must remain vulnerable, honest, and humble. Saying to a child, "I'm sorry" is really not too difficult.

John or I have occasionally said something to our boys out of frustration or a lost temper. When this occurs and I am responsible, I usually get down on their physical level and begin with something like this: "Son, I want to let you know that I sinned against you by saying that. I shouldn't have. I want to be a reflection of your perfect parent—your heavenly Father—and I didn't do a very good job just then. Will you please forgive me?" I have found that my boys are ready to forgive and move on. When parents are transparent with their children about their parenting mistakes, children don't tend to hold grudges.

I believe three things are accomplished when parents are honest with their children when mom or dad has blown it. First, an apology validates the child's perception that something has not gone right, that a violation of their sense of fairness occurred. Second, it demonstrates parental love for them and an honest desire to parent them well. And third, it shows them by example that when failures occur, God is the ultimate, impartial ruler over both parent and child, and the parent should not "lord it over" the child. Counselor Steve Donaldson writes,

> Two characteristics can easily be identified in family therapy that point to health in the parents. The first is the parent's ability to be genuinely humble. Healthy parents...can admit to their failures and the impact these failures have on the child. They do not make excuses for their failures; rather, they are genuinely concerned about the impact on their child. A second characteristic is the parent's ability to tolerate the child's anger. Healthy parents expect children to be angry at them. It's a part of life. Less healthy parents have difficulty allowing this and take it as a personal insult....Healthy parents need little from their children, while unhealthy parents need much.[2]

Fathers

A father's role in affirming his daughter cannot be overstated. It is, beyond a shadow of a doubt, a very powerful role. A girl's father is the first man she falls in love with. She needs to feel adored and protected, not taken advantage of. Her father is then seen as safe and sheltering. Later in life, she will most likely want to find a man like her dad to marry. Instead of seeing marriage as something that threatens her worth as a woman, the daughter sees marriage through the lens of her parents as something desirable and worth working for. By way of contrast, 80 percent of the same-sex attracted women who answered my survey said their parents did not make marriage look desirable.

Okay, I'll admit it...I'm a bit more emotional these days because I'm pregnant as I write this. But as I was reading *She Calls Me Daddy* by Robert Wolgemuth, I found myself in tears. A girl's father has such an important role in her life! Let me give you just a glimpse of what moved me. Mr. Wolgemuth writes:

> This little person [his infant daughter, Missy] was capturing my heart. I couldn't wait to get home from work to look at her and hold her....Late one afternoon, I was lying on the carpeted floor of our living room, cuddled next to her. She was on her tummy, a clean cloth diaper under her head, with her face turned toward me. I studied her tiny features—her velvety skin, little turned-up nose, and rosebud mouth.
>
> As though it were yesterday, I can remember the breathtaking feeling in my soul, not unlike the moment a roller-coaster begins its descent.
>
> "This little girl is my responsibility," I breathed out loud. "I'm her daddy, the only one she'll ever have."
>
> The feeling was overwhelming, but not a frustrated or fearful kind of overwhelmed. I felt resolved. Committed. Ready to tackle the obstacles that would surely lie ahead.

I remember thinking, lying there next to this baby person, *I'll be your daddy, little girl. You can count on me. I can do this. I know I can. God, please help me.*[3]

What an honor and a responsibility are given to a man who is the father of a little girl. Author Gary Smalley says,

There's no challenge for a man quite like being the father of a girl....Boys often love to be tousled and teased by their dads. Girls love to be cherished. Boys can be "spoken to" with single words, half sentences and grunts. Girls want their dads to talk to them in complete sentences. Boys long to live without their dad's protection. Most girls thrive with confidence when they know their dad will be there...I couldn't help but be impressed with the importance honor plays—a dad taking the time to honor his daughter with his love and his time, teaching her to honor and respect him, then helping her to understand the importance of honoring God and others.[4]

The Importance of Siblings

Not only do fathers and mothers have their important roles in forming a child's identity, but even siblings' actions can help support or diminish a child's sense of self. Alexis, Todd and Jennifer's daughter, has had an exceptionally positive experience with her older sister, Stephanie. She told me, "Stephanie is just two years older than me, but she was always like a second mother to me. She included me in everything she did and made me feel awesome about myself. Even in college my sister still encourages me."

Alexis remembers with gratitude how Stephanie made a difference for her when she was 14, during her first year at high school. Alexis had just gone through a couple of socially challenging years in middle school, and her sister took care of her in some pretty thoughtful ways. "I had all my friends set out for me," Alexis recalls. "The freshman year is a hard year and my sister made it so easy for me. I was given motivation to do sports because my sister was in sports. I was following my sister in a lot of ways."

Siblings can magnify either how secure or insecure we already feel about ourselves. When a girl is given a strong foundation from her parents, negative influences from siblings are less likely to wreak havoc. And the positive encouragement and support of sisters and brothers makes facing life's challenges even easier.

When Lisa Beamer was about to receive news from United Airlines about the phone conversation her husband, Todd Beamer, had during the hijacking with an Airfone operator, Lisa went up to her bedroom for the call with the support of her brother. What a support siblings can be in moments of need and tragedy!

Preschool Peer Groups

When discussing the social development of young children, Focus on the Family's *Complete Book of Baby & Child Care* says that a girl's social interaction with peers "will depend, in part, on the flavor of her relationships at home."[5] The manual continues,

> If she is consistently loved and respected, she will be more likely to feel confident and friendly with other children and content to interact with them in a variety of ways. But if she has received the messages that she isn't worth much and that the world in which she lives is dangerous and unpredictable, she may shy away from dealing with other children or may be easily bullied. In the same way, seeing the adults at home overpowering

others with loud voices and threatening actions may inspire her to adopt a similar, aggressive approach to her peers or younger children.[6]

A little girl between preschool and elementary ages who feels good about herself as a girl will prefer "girl" games, make-believe, and dolls, as we have discussed already. She will prefer playing with other girls, mostly because they are interested in similar things. As mentioned at the beginning of the chapter, they can play with boys, but they *prefer* to play with girls.

Later on in this stage, girls label boys as "cooties." The same verdict is returned with great enthusiasm by the boys. I can't tell you how many times I have heard boys say in this stage, "Girls are icky!" with their faces all scrunched up to add extra emphasis. They generally stick to playing with their own gender at this point. Let me give you an example from my son's preschool.

Timmy's preschool dedicated 15 minutes at the beginning to letting the children play with toys in the room. I noticed consistently the unconscious grouping of the boys playing with other boys, focusing on the animals or cars or super-heroes in their imaginations. Sound effects resonated from that cluster. One year, two-thirds of the class was boys, so the day began with *loud* sound effects.

In the other half of the room, the girls grouped together near the play kitchen or near the baby dolls with dress-up clothes. The smaller number of girls was not the only reason that area of the room was always so much calmer. One of the girls was usually directing: "You sit here at the table. Now what would you like to eat?"

I have heard many times, and have said myself, that an invisible line seems to exist between the genders. When the children had the option and felt good about themselves, they would naturally gravitate to members of their same gender. An unseen magnet seemed to draw them together socially.

Elementary School

A popular theme in healthy female gender development from age five through eleven is "girl power." The cartoon *Power Puff Girls,* which emphasizes "girl power," is very popular with this age group of girls. I can almost hear the "humpf!" as a little girl turns her back on an aggressive little boy on the school grounds and walks back to her secure group of girlfriends. Girls often stick together and defend each other at this stage. Hormones and competition have not yet arrived in a powerful way.

In his book *Bringing Up Boys,* Dr. James Dobson shared a letter he received from a nine-year-old girl entitled, "Girls Are More Better than Boys." This young girl proclaimed 31 reasons why she insists girls are better than boys. I will share a portion of the list in her own words:

- Girls chew with their mouths closed.

- Girls have better hand writing.

- Girls are more talented.

- Girls don't pick their nose.

- Girls learn faster.

- Girls don't smell as bad.

- Girls are more smarter.

- Girls get more things that they want.

- Girls are more creative.

- Girls are more attractive.[7]

Dr. Dobson gave the boys a chance to respond in another newsletter and compiled a list of 47 reasons why "boys are more better than girls" from the responses. I will share just a few from the boys' list in their own words.

- Boys can sit in front of a scary movie and not close their eyes once.

- Boys don't have to sit down every time they go (to the bathroom).

- Boys can build better forts than girls.

- Boys are way more cooler.

- Boys don't waste their life at the mall.

- Boys don't make all those wiggaly movmets when they walk.

- Boys don't brade another's hair.

And my personal favorite:

- Boys are proud of their odor.[8]

"By the age of eight, roughly 85 percent of both sexes believe their own sex is best,"[9] writes Dr. Neil Whitehead. He mentions that at this age,

> "No-girls-allowed" activities are common to boys, in the attempt, some psychologists believe, by the boy to consolidate his gender identity following the shift in identification to his father....The peer group has a similar role to that of the same-sex parent. Mixing mainly with their own sex strengthens a child's sense of being male or female, and the differences deepen.[10]

A funny distinction can be seen when boys and girls are playing their own games at this age. I have seen many examples of this myself: When boys are playing basketball and a boy gets hurt, the game goes right on without him. In fact, another boy may jump in to take his place. But girls generally don't act the same way. Usually if one of the girls gets hurt, the whole game stops and the girls all cluster around her. An adult may actually have difficulty getting through the group to see if she is all right.

Neil and Briar Whitehead also write, "Girls, on the other hand, value relationships, and, if a game starts to cause disputes, it is usually abandoned."[11] Remember, from the beginning, women were created for relationships (Genesis 2:18-24). That motivation continues today.

This is also the stage when a little girl will need to know that her parents are there for her, that she has advocates who let her cry and comfort her, and that she has defenders who will take a stand against her enemies. Parents can offer emotional protection for their daughters during difficult times. Here's another example from the book *She Calls Me Daddy*.

> Ashley came running through the family room door one time when she was six years old. She was sobbing between deep gasps. When they had finally calmed her down enough for her to speak, she told them about the little girl across the street—how she had grabbed Ashley's finger painting from school and torn it in half.
>
> "Then I realized," Dave reported, "that my little girl needed no lecture. This was not a teaching opportunity for me." Dave put his newspaper down. He turned to his daughter and opened his arms. He held her until the crying had subsided. He didn't say a thing.
>
> "What dawned on me...was that life was about angry neighbor kids. About injustice. And about consequences. Ashley was crying, and whatever had happened, she was paying for it with her own

tears. She needed safety. Protection. So I gave it to her."[12]

What a world of difference the protection of her father's arms meant at that time. She could cry and be comforted and then be ready to enter the world again. She was strengthened emotionally by her dad's protection. She was blessed to have such a father. Many daughters do not.

Middle School and Puberty

When I was in teacher training, many of us student teachers expected that working with middle school students would be a challenge simply because of the physical, emotional, and social changes associated with puberty. And we weren't disappointed. I also remember that time in my own life, between the ages of 12 and 14, when the social tables turned in unexpected ways. Along with physical changes, my girlfriends became competitive with each other over various boys. Puberty is a very awkward time—and no wonder. Neil and Briar Whitehead succinctly explain the landmarks of puberty in their book *My Genes Made Me Do It*:

> In boys, the body is flooded with the male hormone, testosterone; in girls, the female hormones, estrogen and progesterone. In boys, the voice deepens, the genitals enlarge, and body hair thickens; in girls, breasts develop and menstruation begins. Both become aware of themselves as sexual creatures. Boys experience their first erotic arousal at about age thirteen, and romantic fantasy begins in girls. In heterosexuality, this new sensation is expressed toward the opposite sex. But puberty does not create a sex drive that overrides existing sexual orientations, preferences, attractions, and emotional attachments. The hormonal surge only eroticizes the psychological orientation

that already exists. In people with a developing heterosexual orientation, sexual desire is expressed toward the opposite sex.[13]

Early in a little girl's life, she probably will experiment and identify with femininity by dressing up in Mommy's clothing, shoes, and possibly even makeup. This may also include taking care of others, assuming the play role of Mommy, and mimicking her mother in a myriad of ways. She may even have her own little purse. In preadolescence, a girl who is identifying with her "girlness" will need to be prepared for her upcoming transition to becoming a woman. In other words, she needs to be prepared ahead of time for the physical and emotional changes such as development of breasts, onset of menstruation, the appearance of pubic hair, and the emotional roller coaster that can accompany the hormones that flood her body. She needs the proactive involvement of her mother in providing information and support, as well as shopping together for that first bra and other feminine products.

Alexis had the wonderful opportunity of having a sister, Stephanie, who was two years older. As Stephanie went through this transitional process with her mother, Alexis listened in.

> It was kind of embarrassing—my sister would ask my mom anything while we were driving to or from school, but those conversations prepared me well. When we went shopping for Stephanie's first bra, I went along too and my mom bought me one. When we bought feminine products at the grocery store, I got them too. So I was really prepared years ahead of when I would actually need all those things.

Another family that I know prepared their children very deliberately about a year before they encountered puberty. When their children were in sixth grade, the public school was about to present sexual education material to the children with both boys and girls in the same class. Instead of ceding to the school's plan, my friend Angie and her husband, Tony, instituted their own class.

> My feeling was, if you can talk with your kids about sex and they can talk with you, then they'll talk to you about anything. So we pulled them out of school and chose a curriculum that was fun, that would make them read aloud, and that was built for their age. I taught a small group of four or five girls and my husband taught a group of four or five boys in a separate room. As I shared with the girls about their reproductive systems, I explained, "These are what your body parts are, and it is wonderful how God has designed you." We each explained separately about intercourse and how babies are formed.

Angie's daughter, Isabella, now in her early 20s, remembers the uncomfortable parts of these talks. "It was very disturbing, not that intercourse happens, but that your mother is saying that she *might* have done that. At least twice anyway," Isabella, who has one brother, added with laughter.

High School Years and Boys!

Alexis's life changed dramatically when her body developed. "Before puberty, I was not paid a lot of attention. Then in seventh grade (around 12 years old) puberty hit, and I was no longer flat-chested. Immediately, one of the "popular" boys had a crush on me, and it has been almost non-stop interest from boys since then.

"I remember a time in class," Alexis continued, "when a guy behind me snapped my bra. I stood up immediately and slapped him. I felt very disrespected by him."

"But," I added, "you didn't let him get away with that behavior. Your action let him know that there would be repercussions for his behavior and you would not endure his disrespect."

Isabella had similar experiences. Both girls defended themselves from inappropriate advances from pubescent boys. They were very attractive to the boys around them, and now both are beautiful young women. But they had the ability to assert their dignity and self-respect as girls during their school years.

For example, Isabella, a beautiful brunette with a classic Italian appearance, had a particularly challenging time with one boy at a pool party when she was 15 years old. "This guy wouldn't stop pawing me," she told me. "He just wouldn't leave me alone, and I didn't have a lot of tolerance for that kind of behavior. So I told him that if he didn't stop touching me, I was going to throw him into this stream that was close by. Sure enough, he did it again, so I tossed him into the stream."

Because boys were so drawn to her, Isabella took judo and self-defense classes and began lifting weights.

From the time I was 13, boys had been fawning over me with cat calls, unasked-for attention, and even stalking. When guys were disrespectful to me, I simply didn't have a lot of tolerance for that kind of behavior! My older brother, Josh, got wind of a troublesome boy once and became very protective of me as well. Josh is so likeable, but he is big and told that guy to stop bothering me or else he would have to deal with him. I have also always felt so supported by my parents. I could always go and talk with them and figure out a way to deal with these problems.

Alexis told me how her father protected her in the dating process.

> Dad would interview the guy I was going out with and ask him questions. The one thing that each date told me after the "interview" was how my dad described me. He would say, "My daughter is like a rose to me. She's the most precious thing in my life. Think of something that is precious to you. Well, my daughter is ten times more precious." I would hear that report from every guy that I dated. It was really wonderful to hear that my sister and I were so special to him. It felt very honoring to know that my dad was looking out for my best. Because of this, we knew we meant the world to him.

Each of these sets of parents were clear about communicating the beauty of God's plans and design for marriage to their daughters. They were able to talk to their daughters about sex with respect, conveying the beauty of waiting until marriage to have sex. Both couples declared God's creation in their girls to be "fearfully and wonderfully made" (Psalm 139:13-14).

Each of these girls encountered difficulty in their lives, but they had a foundation of security and strength as girls to stand up to life's challenges.

Now Isabella has found a young man she may marry, a man who treasures her, who does not ask her to compromise her Christian values, a man of strength who also values her strength as a woman. God intends marriage to be a blessing, an intimate and permanent union that can provide the stability necessary for raising healthy children.

A Final Thought

The Bible offers a delightful view into the purposeful design of women in Genesis 2. Women were designed to find worth, value, and fullness in their relationships. This is what Dr. Michael Gurian, author of *The Wonder of Girls,* calls the "intimacy imperative...the hidden yearning in every girl's and woman's life to live in a safe web of intimate relationships."[14]

Given a healthy family environment, certainly not one without problems, little girls naturally desire to imitate their God-given role models—their mothers (or female primary caregivers). They may be able to play with boys and even see themselves as tomboys because they are active and not intimidated by boys, but they limit their identification with boys. Generally—especially up through age ten—girls prefer playing with other girls when given the option.

True feminine beauty is more than skin deep, as the apostle Peter wrote in 1 Peter 3. Women who love God will radiate that beauty with faith in God when experiencing tragedy or standing up for what is right.

Mothers, fathers, and siblings each have their own role in constructing a healthy environment that enables a young girl to become a confident, secure woman. A solid, respectful marital relationship demonstrated between her father and mother goes a long way to securing a daughter's identity as female. Humility in the parenting process adds a necessary dimension of character building in both the parents and the children. Healthy, not perfect, parenting should be any parent's goal in raising a daughter.

In the developmental years preceding puberty, the parents' ability to communicate with and listen to their daughter will build emotional security as she encounters painful realities of the world beyond. A mother who discusses the upcoming changes caused by puberty intelligently and sensitively—before their onset—helps her daughter a great deal.

After the onset of puberty, a girl will need the emotional support of her family as she negotiates a volatile time of life. She still needs the protection and physical and emotional affection of her "daddy," as well as the communication and support of her mother, as her hormones produce tremendous changes throughout her being.

God created woman by design and for His delight. Remember that after God had created both man and woman in His image, He declared His work "very good."

Whether or not she gets married, a young woman needs to understand the beauty of her design by a purposeful God. The Lord God has only the best of intentions for her life. As Jeremiah wrote, "Obey me, and I will be your God and you will be my people. Walk in all the ways I command you, that it may go well with you" (Jeremiah 7:23).

Having a life that "goes well"—isn't that something we *all* want?

5

Establishing a Support System

When God mends a broken life, He often uses the experience of those who have walked a similar path. As the Apostle Paul writes, "Praise be to the God and Father of our Lord Jesus Christ, the Father of compassion and the God of all comfort, who comforts us in all our troubles, *so that we can comfort those in any trouble with the comfort we ourselves have received from God*" (2 Corinthians 1:3-4).

When we've experienced the goodness of God, we want others to know His love too. For that very reason, I would be amiss if I didn't take a few moments and discuss the primary source of healing available to lesbian women—coming to know Christ personally.

If you're a woman dealing with same-sex attraction, the past few chapters may have brought up painful memories or stirred up feelings of loss. In this chapter, I want to offer some good news and affirm the importance of a good support system in the healing process.

God's goal for us—for you and me—is *good*. But many of us are accustomed to being hurt, to having relationships go wrong, to struggling with the pain of our past. We can hardly believe our lives can be better. Nonetheless, many women, including myself, have found a life that is infinitely better than anything we've experienced before as we've responded to Christ's invitation to a new life. We've turned from chasing the illusion of lesbianism to the reality of the only One who can comfort us completely—the Lord Jesus Christ.

Perhaps you've been "in the life" long enough to have discovered that same-sex relationships eventually leave you empty and feeling tremendous loss. Meanwhile, the craving for true intimacy continues to recur. We all share a deep thirst for a satisfying relationship that *lasts*.

I love the story in the gospel of John of Jesus approaching a woman at a well—a woman acquainted with disappointing temporal relationships—and asking her if she would draw Him a drink of water. He told her, "If you knew the gift of God and who it is that asks you for a drink, you would have asked him and he would have given you living water.... Everyone who drinks this water will be thirsty again, but whoever drinks the water I give him will never thirst. Indeed, the water I give him will become in him a spring of water welling up to eternal life" (John 4:10-14).

I can identify with that woman, can't you? If so, perhaps your time has come to abandon the broken wells that have gone dry and drink deeply from the One who offers this living water.

The good news is that through Christ, God has made a way for us to be given a new life. All we have to do is put up the white flag, surrender ourselves to Him, and accept God's provision for our deepest needs—Jesus. From then on, life becomes a process of learning to live through the power of Jesus Christ in us.

If the lesbian lifestyle has left you tired and weighed down, you will delight in the invitation of Christ:

> Come to me, all you who are weary and burdened,
> and I will give you rest. Take my yoke upon you

and learn from me, for I am gentle and humble in heart, and you will find rest for your souls. For my yoke is easy and my burden is light (Matthew 11:28-30).

Through the power and kindness of God, countless lesbian women have found security and delight in their identity as females despite horrendous childhoods and damaging choices in adulthood. These women have also discovered that God is the Great Restorer. He more than makes up for all we've missed while pursuing our lesbian lifestyle. And as if that isn't enough, He then allows us the joy of offering comfort to others who are troubled by the choices they have made.

I hope you have made a decision to follow Christ. All that follows will mean so much more to you if you are a Christian.

The God Who Restores

In the previous chapter we looked at God's purposes for creating men and women. We also saw the importance of a healthy family in the proper development of a young woman's sexual identity.

But what happens when those vital elements are missing? How can a woman make up for the destruction and abuse of her early years, including the years of childhood over which she had no control? Does the absence of a strong family and the likely insecurity that results mean a woman must forever live with the pain that follows? Can a woman who has rejected her female gender assignment from God ever really enter into and *enjoy* being a woman?

Yes! To all those questions—and more. Our God is a God who *restores*. One of the most exciting promises in the Bible for anyone who has undergone extreme emotional pain or loss is found in Joel 2:25-26. God says to his devastated people,

> I will repay you for the years the locust have eaten—
> the great locust and the young locust,
> the other locusts and the locust swarm—
> my great army that I sent among you.
> You will have plenty to eat, until you are full,
> and you will praise the name of the Lord your God,
> who has worked wonders for you;
> never again will my people be shamed.

God gives a new life to everyone who comes to Him. His invitation is to an *abundant* life, not a dismal life with emotional baggage from our past. As the Apostle Paul wrote regarding the Christian life, "Therefore, if anyone is in Christ, he is a new creation; the old has gone, the new has come!" (2 Corinthians 5:17).

As we walk out our new life, we need support. So please don't go on this journey alone. You will need others, and they will need you. God has given us each other to help us through. As Scripture instructs us, "Carry each other's burdens, and in this way you will fulfill the law of Christ" (Galatians 6:2). And again, "And if one member suffers, all the members suffer with it; if one member is honored, all the members rejoice with it. Now you are Christ's body, and individually members of it" (1 Corinthians 12:26-27 NASB).

Help from other Christians is available to us, whether we are new Christians still struggling with same-sex attraction; parents, relatives, or friends of a lesbian; or a pastor or other counselor who wants to learn more about women who must work through their same-sex attraction.

Motivation to Seek Help

Our emotional pain or longing often drives us to seek support from others. Yet even for a parent of a same-sex attracted child, the barriers to seeking wise counsel are numerous: fear of exposing the child, fear of being misunderstood, fear of reputation, not knowing who to turn to, and other related concerns. Opening up enough to obtain appropriate help is sometimes risky. But the following pages are offered to minimize the risks and maximize the rewards.

I've found that a woman who experiences same-sex attraction will often seek help as a result of one or more events in her life:

- breakup of an intensely emotional or sexual relationship with another woman

- an unwanted attraction that seems overpowering

- emotional pain from past abuse

- unfulfilled longings for connection with others

- a difficult relationship at work or church that brings up old wounds, fears, or longings

This is by no means a comprehensive list, but here is an additional key motivation for a woman to seek help: *She feels that her desires are in conflict with her relationship with God.* The Holy Spirit may have been working in His unique and spectacular way, bringing a woman's heart to realize that her feelings and/or actions are in opposition to His will. This supernatural work comes directly from God's Holy Spirit and becomes a woman's own internal motivation for change.

Qualities of Wise Advice

When a woman makes the decision to leave lesbianism for the joys of the Christian life, a mentor, pastor, or long-time friend who is willing to walk alongside her to listen, support, and encourage her can be an invaluable resource as she goes through this process of change.

In the beginning of my journey out of lesbianism, I gleaned a great deal from a woman who was willing to care

He who walks with the wise grows wise, but a companion of fools suffers harm (Proverbs 13:20).

for me and journey with me. She was Anita Worthen, the mother of a gay son and wife of Frank Worthen, who helped to found Exodus International—the world's largest network of Christian ministries helping men and women leave homosexuality.

Anita admitted freely, "I don't have all the answers." But she listened and learned from the women who came to her for help. What a profound difference she made in my own life. Had I discounted her advice and care simply because she had not personally overcome homosexuality, I would have missed a great deal of what God wanted to do in my life!

The key is to allow God to direct you to a wise counselor or mentor. In order to discern wise advice from foolish, let's see what the book of Proverbs has to say. Wisdom is shown by...

- listening and learning (Proverbs 1:5)

- accepting advice, rebuke, and instruction (Proverbs 9:8-9; 10:8; 12:15)

- fearing the Lord and avoiding evil (Proverbs 14:16)

- words that promote healing, instruction, and reverence of God (Proverbs 12:18; 13:14)

A wise woman could be defined as someone who has humbled herself in order to learn from others, has internalized God's love and law, has trained her heart to listen to correction, is able to teach others, and speaks words that are trustworthy and true. As Scripture says, her words promote healing, but she does not ignore conflict, nor promote fiery situations (Proverbs 29:8).

So what are the benefits of seeking wise counsel? First, we will also become wise as we listen and learn. Wisdom, to personified, counsels us to:

Choose my instruction instead of silver, knowledge rather than choice gold, for wisdom is more precious than rubies, and nothing you desire can compare with her....Counsel and sound judgment are mine; I have understanding and power....I love those who love me, and those who seek me find me. With me are riches and honor....For whoever finds me finds life and receives favor from the LORD. But whoever fails to find me harms himself; all who hate me love death (Proverbs 8:10-11,14, 17-18, 35-36).

Many other important blessings result from listening to wisdom:

- inheriting honor (Proverbs 3:35)

- bringing joy to others (Proverbs 10:1; 14:35)

- gaining the protection of wisdom (Proverbs 14:3)

- winning souls (Proverbs 11:30)

...and many more. (To find all of wisdom's benefits, you may wish to take a few minutes each day to read through a chapter of the Book of Proverbs and jot your notes in a notebook. You will complete the book in one month!)

We must understand that listening implies obedience. Again and again in Scripture, the Lord implores: "If my people would but listen to me, if Israel would follow my ways..." (Psalm 81:13). In contrast, not listening implies rebellion or disobedience: "But you would not listen. You rebelled against the LORD's command" (Deuteronomy 1:43).

I have often used this example of listening with my boys. Many times I have told them, "Please put on your shoes, it's time to leave for school. *Boys, are you listening?*"

Of course, they answered, "Yes, Mom." But I don't want them to simply listen to my request, I want them to follow my instructions. By putting on their shoes, they show they've truly listened.

Do you want to be wise? Then you must listen to and be ready to obey God's Word.

> He who listens to a life-giving rebuke will be at home among the wise. He who ignores discipline despises himself, but whoever heeds correction gains understanding. The fear of the LORD teaches a man wisdom, and humility comes before honor (Proverbs 15:31-33).

Where to Look for Help

Maybe this all sounds good to you, but you aren't sure to whom you should listen. Who can be trusted? I would recommend pursuing several avenues of support, starting with already developed resources and then expanding your search in reliable ways.

Your Church and Pastor

If you're already established in a church, consider making an appointment with your pastor. If your church has a women's counselor, you might try an appointment with her. But be forewarned: We who are ministering in this area have often run into roadblocks of denial from the pastorate. "Oh, no one is struggling with same-sex attraction in my church!" How very wrong they often are!

Pastors and church leaders should do some research in this area. I know of several pastors who had no idea how to help members of their congregations who asked for help with same-sex issues. You can help your pastor by recommending other resources to him. You may even wish to come to your appointment with your pastor with some helpful materials, such as this book.

Jessica is a young woman who did just that. She made an appointment to speak with her pastor about her same-sex attracted sister. She wasn't sure what to expect in the way of support, but she took along some written testimonies from the Exodus International newsletter, *Exodus Update*, as well as several books.

"My pastor had more questions than I anticipated," Jessica shared with me, "but that also was very encouraging. I left the meeting feeling that he had listened to me and had committed to reading and learning along with me about relating to my sister. In kind of a medical scenario, I felt like I had met with a family physician and obtained his support, rather than a specialist. More immediate and frequent care is given by the family physician. His support meant a lot to me."

The Christian church is to be a safe haven for the wounded heart. For those who long for family, who have missed out in childhood, God provides a new family—the Body of Christ, those who believe Jesus is the Son of God and are in the process of reflecting Jesus to the world. Our attitude toward the needy should be the same as God's: "*A father to the fatherless, defender of widows, is God in his holy dwelling. God sets the lonely in families, he leads forth the prisoners with singing; but the rebellious live in a sun-scorched land*" (Psalm 68:5-6).

But even as we seek support in our local churches, we need to keep our eyes open for warning signs that our church leaders may not be the best source of help: messages constantly discouraging Christians from seeking counseling from Christian professionals, lack of vulnerability, and lack of interpersonal skills.

Let me give you another positive example. When I first became a Christian at age 18, I went to the pastor of my college group and asked for help in dealing with my homosexuality. Pastor Bob was a wonderful orator, a gifted debater in the secular community, and an incredible teacher, but he was not a counselor.

"Anne," Pastor Bob shared, "I'm so glad you came to me, but I'm not gifted in the area of counseling. However, I can refer you to a local pastor who is both gifted and trained in this area. Would you like me to give you his number?"

Every now and then, Pastor Bob would ask me, "Anne, how is the counseling going? Are you finding it helpful?"

The outcome of that important dialogue was that I was given the best of both worlds—a wonderfully supportive pastor and an excellent outlet to pursue help. Both continued to be strong supports and helped me grow significantly.

Friends

If you sense that going to the pastor or church counselor is not safe, you may turn to friends who have been tried and true. Friends who offer to walk alongside you as you learn how to deal with same-sex attraction are valuable friends indeed!

How can you know if a friend is trustworthy?

- She doesn't reveal personal confidences about others.

- She is someone who has gone through difficulty in her own life. My husband often says, "I don't trust anyone who hasn't been broken."

- She doesn't think she knows everything but is willing to listen to you, care for you, and learn along with you.

- Also, she is not someone who is still in the throes of lesbianism or who may take advantage of your vulnerability.

I would even recommend sharing with more than one friend, particularly if you have quality friendships. If you do not have sound friendships, then look to other resources. (Additional discussion of healthy female friendships is included in chapter 8.)

Remember that a woman's sexual orientation does not determine effectiveness as a listener and a friend. One woman, Cheryl, told me with great hesitation about the responses of her family members after she disclosed that she was working through a problem with same-sex attraction. She had shared with them that she was leaving a sexual relationship with a married woman to follow God. Sadly, the wife of her brother saw the disclosure as a way to experiment with lesbianism by exploiting Cheryl's vulnerability. Cheryl wanted to meet with me because she felt helpless to defend herself and establish boundaries. This is rare, but I wish I could say that this was the only occasion that I have heard this type of story.

Still, my own experience with friends and my church was a helpful one. I found support for my decision to obey God and walk out of lesbianism. My hope is that you will experience that same support within the Christian church.

Mentors

Another important source of support may be mentors or disciplers. These relationships may be established with small group leaders, Bible study leaders, or a discipleship program within your church. Using the same criteria mentioned for pastors and friends, you can evaluate the safety factor. For some, these lay leaders may be valuable resources—particularly if you have had some chance to get to know them before sharing this special area of need.

These individuals may help you think through what the Bible says about human sexuality and homosexuality, pray for you, pray with you, and ask you how things are going in this area of your life. A woman should mentor another woman, but always remember to establish personal boundaries clearly. Quite often women leaders have difficulty with setting appropriate and clear boundaries.

So here are a few helpful guidelines for both a mentor and a woman affected by same-sex attraction:

- First, set up meeting times, including both starting and ending times. This will help avoid burnout for the mentor and help a woman not lean solely on that source for help.

- Second, at the conclusion of your first session, assign research to the one with whom you are meeting. This research can include reading specific Scripture passages, journaling thoughts and feelings, and reading other useful materials. This reminds the mentor that the weight of change isn't on her shoulders and encourages the one seeking help to "lift up her eyes" to the One who provides hope.

- Third, minimize phone calls and one-on-one visits outside the meeting times. Remember, the woman needing help should establish a broad base of support. Friends and other forms of support will pick up the slack. Do not discount the danger of developing an overly emotional bond with each other in this setting. If you are a mentor to a woman affected by same-sex attraction, please read about emotional dependency and defensive detachment in chapter 8. This will help you understand the importance of this strong suggestion.

If you are being mentored, you can demonstrate respect for the one helping you by honoring her independence, respecting her time with her family, and agreeing upon times when you may call her. Don't call in the middle of the night or too early in the morning. Rather, ask her when you should call. Even when you agree upon a time, show your respect when calling by asking her, "Is this a convenient time to talk?" You never know if she is sending her children off to school, making lunch, or concluding a conversation with someone else. Hopefully, she will be there for you at the agreed-upon time, but I recommend that you ask anyway.

The very best combination that I have heard of for female same-sex attracted women was shared with me by another female Exodus counselor.[1] When looking for a common denominator of healthy female mentoring relationships, the staff realized that pairing a same-sex attracted woman with a healthy married couple provided the strongest support system. That not only prevented the mentor from falling into a trap of codependency but also gave the women a new view of how women should be treated by men. The husband had the very important role of showing how a man can cherish his wife.

Christian Support Groups

Exodus International is the largest network of Christian support for individuals affected by homosexuality. Exodus is based in Orlando, Florida, and is a coalition of ministries from a variety of denominations, nondenominational churches, and parachurch organizations. Many of the local ministries are run by individuals who have moved on from homosexuality or same-sex attraction themselves. They all believe that change is possible—from the inside out. In other words, change is not just about behavior, but it's about much more—the transformation of a person's identity. And Exodus counselors have the personal life stories to prove their point!

Other support groups also exist in the United States and abroad. Courage is the

Courage
www.couragerc.net
(212) 268-1010
c/o Church of St. John the Baptist
210 West 31st Street
New York, NY 10001
email: NYCourage@aol.com

Catholic support group for change from homosexuality and same-sex attraction. Homosexuals Anonymous applies a 12-step program to change behavior and measures success in the form of "sexual sobriety." Jonah is the Jewish ministry that cares for those affected by homosexuality. Many other support groups may be available through your specific denomination as well. Most of these affiliate to some degree with Exodus International and can be located by contacting the Exodus office [see sidebar].

Living Waters is another good resource. Desert Stream Ministries, an affiliate of Exodus based out of Anaheim, California, developed the Living Waters curriculum and training program for churches to help with all areas of sexual brokenness. The Living Waters program has spread literally around the world and is an excellent avenue for change.

You may be surprised to learn how many different support groups for same-sex strugglers exist! *Help is available.* I encourage you to persist in looking for assistance until an opportunity opens up for you. For contact information for some of the resources I've mentioned, see the sidebars on pages 111-113.

Exodus International
(406) 599-6872
PO Box 540119
Orlando, FL 32854
www.exodus-international.org

Homosexuals Anonymous Fellowship Services
(610) 921-0345
PO Box 7881
Reading, PA 19603
www.members.aol.com/hawebpage

JONAH
Jews Offering New Alternatives to Homosexuality
(201) 433-3444
PO Box 313
Jersey City, NJ 07303
www.jonahweb.org

Educational Conferences

In addition to support groups, many conferences are designed to help same-sex strugglers.

Focus on the Family's one-day Love Won Out conference is focused on "addressing, understanding, and preventing homosexuality" and is hosted in different cities around the United States at least four times a year. For information, you can call 800 A FAMILY (800-232-6459) and ask for details about Love Won Out, or you can visit their website at www.lovewonout.org.

Every summer Exodus International North America hosts a powerful week-long conference for leaders and those struggling with homosexuality. This conference varies its location within the U.S. from year to year but always incorporates workshops, plenary sessions, worship, and opportunities to get connected with others dealing with same-sex attractions. I would highly recommend both of these vital conferences.

Educational Resources

Exodus and Focus on the Family also publish additional materials on the topic of same-sex attraction and homosexuality. Some materials are addressed to pastors, teens, parents, or family and friends. Regeneration Books is the official bookseller for Exodus materials and can be located on the Web at www.exodus-international.org/resources. Focus on the Family resources can be purchased through the mail (Focus on the Family, Colorado Springs, CO 80995), on the Internet at www.family.org, or by phone at 800 A FAMILY. (For hearing impaired/deaf, the TDD phone is [877] 877-0503).

Fortunately, more books addressing this issue from a Christian perspective are becoming available in many bookstores.

Desert Stream Ministries
www.desertstream.org
(714) 779-6899
PO Box 17635
Anaheim, CA 92817-7635
email: info@desertstream.org

NARTH
www.narth.com
(818) 789-4440
16633 Ventura Blvd., St. 1340
Encino, CA 91436-1801

Professional Christian Counselors and Professional Secular Counselors

To find a professional counselor in your area, contact Focus on the Family or Exodus International for a referral to a Christian therapist. Or you can call NARTH (National Association for Research and Therapy of Homosexuality), a secular network of professionals who believe in the therapeutic process as a means to resolve same-sex attraction. If you are attending a church, you may wish to ask your pastor or a counselor friend for a local referral.

Unfortunately, outside of these references, many counselors, social workers, psychologists, and psychiatrists now believe that change from homosexuality is not possible. They believe this *not* because of facts (as discussed in chapter 2) but because of the persuasiveness of the gay lobby, false media declarations, and the threat of being labeled homophobic or bigoted within their professional associations.

Because of the pressure from within their associations, these individuals may attempt to persuade you that you shouldn't pursue change in regard to your sexual attractions. Many therapists seem to value sexual expression above the client's personal belief system and would rather attempt to persuade you to change your beliefs than provide the help you really want. For example, The American Academy of Pediatrics has concluded in their policy statement, "Homosexuality and Adolescence," "Therapy directed specifically at changing sexual orientation is contraindicated, since it can produce guilt and anxiety while having little or no potential to change."[2]

However, this statement did not take into account the many recent studies that contradict that very premise. Several studies have shown a 30 percent change success rate or higher (Nicolosi, Byrd, & Potts, 2000; Spitzer, 2001).[3] Is anyone discouraging alcoholic or drug treatment programs with reported success rates of much less than 30 percent?

In fact, read what therapist Steven Donaldson wrote on this very topic:

> In every major study conducted on rates of change
> for reorientation therapy, success has been
> reported. In fact, patients of therapy report change
> rates that are as good or better than almost any

other psychological difficulty treated by psychotherapy. This includes things like alcohol addiction, drug addiction, clinically significant depression, and anxiety. What is more impressive is that the changes are not in behavior alone but in sexual desires and fantasies."[4]

How to Interview a Counselor

Most mental health professions follow a basic principle of ethics that patients or clients have the right to "self-determination." In other words, if you tell a counselor that you desire change from homosexuality, that counselor is obligated to help you or refer you to someone who can and will help you. Both the American Psychological Association and the National Association of Social Workers agree. But don't rely on that promise. Make sure you and a counselor are working together with the same purpose in mind.

You may wish to ask any therapist these questions at the beginning of your relationship:

- Do you believe that men and women are "born gay"?

- Do you believe that wanting to leave homosexuality is harmful or dangerous?

- Do you believe that change is even possible?

- Can you support me in my desire to change?

- Have you read relevant research concerning the topics of gender identity disorder, homosexuality, and family structure?

If you hear answers that clearly lead you to the conclusion that this counselor—even a Christian counselor—cannot support your goals, you should consider asking for a referral or seeking out another counselor.

Mosaic Counseling Associates also recommends, "Don't see a counselor that is a member of your social circle such as a friend or a person who socializes with the same people you socialize with. Although it does not appear to be a problem in the beginning this can interrupt therapy down the road."[5] They also recommend trusting your intuition. "If you don't get a good feeling about someone there may be a good reason." Additionally, "Shop around. Some counselors will talk with you on the telephone, or even see [you] for a session free of charge."

For information about types of education and licensure, you may wish to visit the website of Mosaic Counseling Associates (www.mosaiccounseling.com). They also discuss types of therapy, costs of counseling, and tools for finding a good counselor. For additional questions to ask a potential counselor, you may wish to visit the website of Institute for Sexual Integrity, www.sexualintegrity.org.

Now that we know where to look for help, let's learn how to help others help you!

Your Motivation

Change always begins with motivation. Are you feeling pressure from others to change, or are you self-motivated? Clearly, your progress will depend on your desire to change. If you don't wish change from same-sex attractions or the lesbian orientation, you will soon go your own way. Your emotions may swing this way and that, but you need to ask yourself, Do I want to change?

Another good question to ask yourself is, What am I pursuing—Jesus or change? I suppose the question might be better worded, What is first in my life, the Lord of all creation or my pursuit of change from homosexuality? Jesus stated our highest calling: "Love the Lord your God with all your heart and with all your soul and with all your mind. This is the first and greatest commandment" (Matthew 22:37-38). Overcoming same-sex behavior, attractions, and identity is ultimately a by-product of following Jesus through difficult times. He is enough to carry us through those moments that challenge our allegiance.

I remember when painful areas of my past drove me to feel powerful attractions toward nurturing women in my life. The only thing I could do was to "hang on to Jesus" with all my might while my world seemed to spin around me. I remembered that when many of Jesus' followers deserted him, Peter responded, "Lord, to whom shall we go? You have the words of eternal life" (John 6:68). And a woman who had unsuccessfully tried every other solution to her problems believed that Jesus had the power to heal her. "She came up behind him and touched the edge of his cloak, and immediately her bleeding stopped" (Luke 8:44). When the process of change seemed too big for me, I purposefully reached out to touch the "hem of his garment."

I've found that women (and men) who pursue change as their first goal often give up too soon. As a result, some who have tried to change are now publicly proclaiming the *impossibility* of change. But one might ask, If some do not experience change in feelings or actions, should we invalidate the experience of thousands of lives that *do* change?

I repeat: Healing, or change from same-sex attraction, is the result of a life committed to following Jesus Christ. We must choose to follow Jesus when we are tempted and when we are not. Besides, I have learned a much higher principle: God does not want *only* the area of homosexuality in your life. He wants you—*all of you.*

Realistic Change

What can those who desire to obey God and want to keep God in first place expect? *Change is not necessarily the absence of homosexual temptation but rather the power to choose our response to temptation.* Is same-sex attraction irresistible? If so, change is only just beginning.

Inner change that lasts includes adopting a new identity, acknowledging the truth about self, God, and others, and becoming the woman that God designed you to be. It does not require that you marry and have a family.

The process of inward transformation usually takes a lot of time. The Bible calls this process *sanctification.* Sanctification can happen in both a moment (separation to God) and in a process (the course of life befitting those so separated).[6]

How long does transformation take? That can vary a great deal with each woman. Many find their response to temptation and, more importantly, their inward identity change significantly in a relatively short period of time. Yet we are all unique creations. We each have unique weaknesses and strengths that can help or hinder God's work in our life.

The depth of our involvement in same-sex fantasies or relationships influences the change process. Women who had a brief experience in childhood and then moved on to adult heterosexual involvement, and women who have been almost exclusively heterosexual and then engaged in an adult same-sex relationship, will probably experience resolution relatively quickly. Those who have had long-term involvement in same-sex activities or fantasy may experience a longer process.

The underlying drive of your sexual attraction toward other women also affects the rate of change. The truth is that same-sex attraction is not purely sexual. A woman's attraction to other women is usually a response to her own deep needs. These needs are not found on the surface of one's thoughts or experiences, but rather they are usually bound up with emotionally painful events and wrong conclusions. God, in His great wisdom, knows when to bring such experiences to the surface so that they can be dealt with. I found this part of the process best likened to unpeeling an onion—

the onion has many more layers than we can initially see, but they appear one at a time.

As Bob Davies and Lori Rentzel wrote in *Coming Out of Homosexuality*, additional factors play a role as well: "your participation in the process of change" and "God's sovereignty."

> For example, one former lesbian joined a support group for recovering homosexuals, then spent many hours each day poring over the handouts and her Bible, entering insights into her journal and praying with her new friends in the group. Three years after her last lesbian relationship, she was happily married and feeling secure in her new identity.[7]

This was similar to my experience. But I am aware of women who have walked through a very similar process of change but took much longer to feel secure as women.

Let me give you a brief list of realistic expectations:

■ You will grow personally, learn about the motivations of your homosexual longings, and gain ground in obeying God.

■ You will experience greater power or authority over your own feelings.

■ God will honor your obedience in a supernatural way, changing your inward perceptions and outward perspectives. Changing your heart is God's work, not yours (Jeremiah 17:9,14).

■ Given hard work, obedience, faith, and perseverance, you will change over time.

■ You will see yourself as being just another woman among women of all types.

What are unrealistic expectations?

■ You will never experience same-sex attracted feelings again. In fact, the Bible promises that we will always encounter temptation this side of heaven (Romans 6:11-14,19-23; 7:14–8:14; also 1 Corinthians 10:13).

■ The intensity of attraction will lessen as we work with God on the underlying issues of our lives. Quite the opposite often happens—as we face our difficulties, attractions seem to offer us a pseudo-anesthetic.

I've noticed that over time the intensity and frequency of sexual attraction to other women lessens significantly—a topic we'll discuss more completely in chapter 7.

Is Change Really Possible?

My personal experience, detailed in my autobiography, *Love Won Out,* shows that change is most certainly possible.[8] My discussions with hundreds of women during more than 17 years of experience in this field confirm that change is possible. The literature on both sides of the issue document that change is possible.

I have met only about six couples where both the man and woman left homosexuality and are married to each other. Most of the lesbians who have resolved same-sex attraction and married a man fell in love with an "ever-straight" man. Remember, marriage is not a measure of change. But for some of us, dealing with our same-sex attracted issues resulted in an interest in the opposite sex and eventual marriage.

I personally know countless women who have resolved same-sex attractions and may desire marriage but have not yet experienced the magical combination with a desirable male. These single women have experienced authentic change just as surely as have married women. Other single women who have experienced change find a lessened attraction toward other members of their sex but no emerging heterosexual attraction. Others were involved with women during their marriage years and have since resolved homoerotic feelings and behaviors. All these women are evidence that change is possible!

The psychological literature on this topic divides according to two strong views. Generally speaking, one is biased toward integrating a gay identity and does not validate change research of any kind. The other view better understands religious viewpoints and evaluates the data differently.

As Dr. Mark Yarhouse, a licensed clinical psychologist at Regent University, states,

> Many gay-affirmative theorists argue that therapy cannot change sexual orientation or that, at least, there is no evidence to date that therapy can change sexual orientation....Conservative religious persons who have looked at the change research have argued that sexual orientation does not appear to be immutable (Satinover, 1996). Recent research by MacIntosh (1994) has challenged the claim of the absolute immutability of sexual orientation.[9]

Another researcher, Dr. Warren Throckmorton, recently published a paper in the journal of the American Psychological Association, *Professional Psychology: Research and Practice.* In his article, Dr. Throckmorton details these arguments and studies of change. In his report of the recent study by Dr. Robert Spitzer,[10] Throckmorton writes, "Spitzer concluded that the majority of the participants made substantial changes from predominantly or exclusively homosexual to predominate heterosexual adjustment."

Dr. Throckmorton also noted that change was "positively associated with religious motivation and emotional well-being." Again and again, mental health researchers and professionals who have examined the issue of change affirm that religious belief systems make a tremendous difference in the change process. Indeed, Dr. Throckmorton concluded, "Clearly the review above suggests that religious belief is often crucial to both the decision to seek change and the maintenance of change"[11] (See also Schaeffer, et al., 2000).[12]

A Word to the Support Person

Those who help women who experience same-sex attraction do well to remember that homosexual attraction is not essentially sexual. It is developmental. Many different outcomes can occur as a result of a woman's early emotional trauma or wrong perceptions about her identity—one of which (lesbianism) is an unhealthy bonding with other women. The roots or underlying issues are quite often the same for many symptoms that women (or men) struggle with. Keep in mind that a lesbian is not a "special" sinner; rather, she's expressing her legitimate needs to connect with other women in an unhealthy manner.

Because of her need to connect with other women in a healthy way, a woman seeking change should meet with a woman counselor or support person. Men can be helpful, but her main problem with bonding correctly is with women. A man simply cannot model healthy female relationships. On the other hand, if she already has a female mentor, she may desire to meet with a male pastor or counselor to work through issues with men. But same-sex attracted women absolutely need to work through relationships with women.

Women counselors and mentors should keep in mind that we, as women, can be prone to codependency. God designed us women to be relational, but codependency is the fallen flip side to our God-ordained natures. Take a good look at your motivations for being in her life. Are you drawn consistently to those who need you? Have you established healthy time, phone, and physical boundaries that will keep you from becoming dependent on your counselee or the woman you are mentoring?

A helpful mentor or counselor is trustworthy, does not gossip, and is willing to learn. A woman seeking help must feel that you care about her welfare without crossing established boundaries.

Above all, *she* must be motivated to change. You must not take personally her "failures" along the way. If she enters a sexual relationship with another woman, she is not rejecting you. She is responsible to One person for her life—the Lord Jesus Christ. Be a good and supportive listener as she walks forward with God into being a complete, whole woman. Keep in mind that the road to changing sexual attraction and identity can be a long and difficult one and that you are there for a specific season in her life. You are not her Savior.

Those who help in a counseling or support group setting will most likely encounter a natural emotional progression. At first, a needy person may see you as not understanding her at all. Then, as you build trust with her, her perspective may shift to believing that you perfectly understand her. Both the disconnected and completely attached conclusions are false. At some point, you will probably fall off the pedestal she has placed you on, which may feel a bit distressing to you. But the truth is more likely that you understand some things about her and want to help her. The distorted pendulum may swing too far either way.

Believe it or not, the goal is for the Lord to bring up any unresolved issue or conclusion in her life, so you may find yourself triggering a past wound unintentionally. If you are responsible for hurting her, apologize, but if she has an intensely painful response, keep in mind that you may have touched something painful from the past. Asking her if these feelings bring up anything from the past may be quite enlightening. If something does emerge in this process, be willing to listen, pray, and empathize with her.

Also, if you feel completely over your head in your helping relationship with a same-sex attracted woman, you can always refer to a professional Christian therapist or support group in your area. Some Exodus ministries offer e-mail counseling as well.

Most of the women who responded to my survey (67 percent) have dealt with some form of depression, and one-quarter have attempted suicide. Other typical symptoms for this group tend to go along with self-medicating depression: overeating, alcoholism, and chemical dependency. Much rarer were cases of anorexia and bulimia. Severe depression, suicidal thoughts, and extreme forms of personal abuse should lead you to refer the individual to professional help, as should symptoms of serious mental health issues, such as borderline personality disorder, disassociative disorder, or paranoid schizophrenia.

But, I must add, symptoms of dependency coming from the woman you are helping is a *good* sign. She needs to have a safe place to bond with another woman and work past her attractions. If you have established good boundaries, such as meeting in an office setting for an hour once a week, you should be a safe woman to experience those powerful feelings with and to dialogue through with her. However, I do not recommend this in a situation where the relationship is primarily friendship or where the helper is being drawn into attraction as well.

6

$\mathcal{H}$ealing from $\mathcal{A}$buse

I first met Christine, a 20-year-old blonde Florida girl, in San Antonio, Texas, in the summer of 1989. We were both beginning to deal with our same-sex attractions and met attending our first Exodus Annual Conference. After the general sessions, we met with others to sing worship songs and talk. Since then, God has done unbelievably incredible things in both of our lives.

But life wasn't always so wonderful for Christine. She recounted her life story in a February, 2001 issue of *Christian Single:*

> While growing up in my parents' home, I noticed that women were either the object of a man's lust or the victim of his abuse. There was no in between. My father had stacks of pornographic magazines under his bed and he routinely hit my mother.
>
> Late one night when I was 4 years old, a scene unfolded that haunted me for years. I laid in bed with the covers pulled over my head, trying to block out the angry voices coming from the next room. I couldn't sleep with all the yelling, so I tiptoed out of

Speak up for those who cannot speak for themselves, for the rights of all who are destitute (Proverbs 31:8).

my bedroom and down the hall where I peered into the living room. Dad was glaring at Mom with a cold, angry look. Then he raised a tennis racket and swung at her, hitting the left side of her body. She stood there motionless and did not fight back.

Tears stained my pillow that night as I vowed in my heart never to let a man hurt me like that. Watching their abusive marriage, I determined not to be a victim like my mom. I believed that to be feminine was to be weak and passive. I wanted no part of it.[1]

What painful experiences for both mother and daughter! Christine's mother was caught in a cycle of abuse and codependency, and Christine was learning lessons that would impact her life for years to come.

This story demonstrates the impact of witnessing the abuse of a family member. How much greater is the impact of experiencing childhood abuse!

How Common Is Childhood Abuse Among Lesbians?

When I conducted my survey of women overcoming same-sex attraction, I strongly suspected that childhood abuse might have played a role in their lives.[2] What surprised me was the incredibly high incidence of childhood abuse reported by the women. In fact, out of the 265 respondents, only 23 reported *not* experiencing abuse in childhood. In other words, 91.2 percent reported abusive childhood experiences!

Not all women reported experiencing the same form of abuse, and some experienced several forms of childhood trauma.

- Almost seventy percent reported experiencing emotional abuse.

- two-thirds, sexual abuse

- more than one-half, verbal abuse

- almost forty percent, abandonment

- one-third, physical abuse

- one-quarter, neglect

- twenty percent, spiritual abuse

The chart below tracks this frequency of abuse. Because some women reported multiple forms of childhood abuse, the total of the numbers across the columns will be much higher than 265 (the number of women surveyed).

Childhood Abuse Experienced

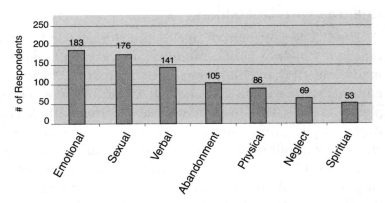

In addition, two-thirds of these women also witnessed the abuse of a family member! The primary forms witnessed were: physical (almost 60 percent), verbal, and emotional (almost one-half each).[3]

These findings differ markedly from the national averages of reported abuse. In a report by the U.S. Department of Justice in November of 2000, 17.6 percent of all women surveyed said that "they had been the victim of a completed or attempted rape at some time in their life."[4] Note the contrast between their survey and mine: almost 18 percent over *an entire lifetime* for this population of women versus my survey's finding of almost a 65 percent victimization rate before the age of 18.

Furthermore, the U.S. Department of Health and Human Services reports that abuse rates for females under the age of 18 *totaled* 12.5 percent in 1999.[5] This figure includes all state reports for the following types of abuse during 1999: neglect, physical, sexual, medical, and psychological. They may seem low when compared to 90 percent of the women in my survey, but U.S. Health and Human Services rates reflect state awareness and intervention and are therefore underestimating abuse nationwide simply because abuse is under-reported to authorities. Taking all of those considerations into account, the reported experience of childhood abuse for the women who later dealt with same-sex attraction is still extremely high.

Children with Disabilities

The U.S. Department of Health and Human Services also reports, "Children with disabilities are more vulnerable to maltreatment than children without disabilities."[6] The only national study to date (Crosse, Kaye & Ratnofsky) was completed in 1993. The study found that children with disabilities were 1.7 times more likely to be maltreated than children without disabilities. The publication also reported that neglect is the most common form of maltreatment of children with disabilities.[7] In addition, it addressed the relationship between the form of disability and the type of abuse. The research found that children with behavioral disorders were at highest risk, followed by children with speech/language disorders, mental retardation, and health impairments.[8]

Some researchers have hypothesized that a greater percentage of individuals in the deaf community deal with homosexuality or same-sex attraction than in the general hearing population. Could that be related to the fact that their disability puts them at greater risk of abuse and/or the greater difficulty of connecting securely with their parents?

What Are the Costs of Abuse?

The devastating short- and long-term results of abuse have been well documented by the U.S. government and by professionals within the health industries. The National Clearinghouse on Child Abuse and Neglect Information reports,

> Child abuse and neglect have known detrimental effects on the physical, psychological, cognitive, and behavioral development of children (National Research Council, 1993). These consequences range from minor to severe and include physical injuries, brain damage, chronic low self-esteem, problems with bonding and forming relationships, developmental delays, learning disorders, and aggressive behavior. Clinical conditions associated with abuse and neglect include depression, post-traumatic stress disorder, and conduct disorders.... Beyond the trauma inflicted on individual children, child maltreatment also has been linked with long-term, negative societal consequences. For example, studies associate child maltreatment with increased risk of low academic achievement, drug use, teen pregnancy, juvenile delinquency, and adult criminality (Widom, 1992; Kelly, Thornberry, and Smith, 1997).[9]

Residual Effects of Physical Abuse

Many women who experience same-sex attractions will also deal with some of these other results. One friend of mine became a Christian just over five years ago and left her lesbian lover to follow Jesus. Her childhood had been terrible—her father physically abused her and her siblings. Both parents placed unreasonable expectations on the children, and if they seemingly failed, the parents belittled them with verbal and emotional abuse. And that was just the tip of the iceberg.

Julie is a high-functioning individual who is both street-smart and sophisticated. She is able to work with everyday people as well as leaders of organizations. I will never forget a time when we were having a cookout at my house and I reached out to pat her on the shoulder. She flinched as if I was going to hit her! I felt so terrible for her. That was just one residual area left from physical abuse of the past. Julie also currently struggles with bonding to others, forming intimate friendships, and trusting others enough to be accountable. But, thankfully, she recognizes her problems and is investing in her own healing through counseling.

Residual Effects of Neglect

Grace, a friend and former roommate of mine who also dealt with same-sex attraction issues, came from a background of both neglect and sexual abuse. As an example, she didn't learn the simple dental hygiene of brushing her teeth until she began junior high school. Unfortunately, many of her baby teeth had rotted by then. She was also allowed to wander around her small town unsupervised from about the age of eight. Several years later, when she was a sophomore in high school, Grace went to visit her cousin for the summer and returned home to find that her family had moved to another city. They had not even thought to call and tell her they were moving. Generations of neglectful parenting in her family had opened the door to sexual abuse as well. A cousin, uncle, or other male extended family member had molested many of the children in the family, boys and girls alike. In fact, Grace's mother had been raped by her grandfather when she was a teenager.

Healthy physical touch was absent in Grace's childhood. Her father must have known about his children's sexual abuse because once when Grace was very young, he held her on his lap and told her, "I will never hurt you." From that comment, Grace assumed he meant he would not sexually abuse her. That sweet moment of being embraced by her loving father ended abruptly when he accidentally fell into an exposed stove pipe, resulting in serious burns on his arm and the withdrawal of her father's touch.

Later in life, Grace had a series of exclusively same-sex intimate relationships where she could experience touch in a pleasant way, although she never considered herself a lesbian. And then over a period of time, after dealing with many of the issues underlying her same-sex attractions, she was able to marry a loving husband and start her own family. That does not mean that the consequences of her childhood are gone completely, but rather Grace has moved on successfully enough to trust men and nurture her children.

The consequences of neglect on children have been studied and documented in a publication entitled *Short- and Long-Term Consequences of Neglect,* published by the National Clearinghouse on Child Abuse and Neglect Information. The report states,

> Social learning theory has also been employed to explain the differences that are found between abused and neglected children. Neglected children appear to be more generally passive and socially withdrawn in their interactions with peers, whereas abused children are more aggressive and active.... [Neglected preschool children] were the least creative in seeking solutions....They were distractible and hyperactive, reluctant to seek help, and showed the most negative and least positive effect of the children. They were also the least persistent in problem solving. Physically neglected children suffered the most severe developmental consequences of the four maltreated groups of children

studied—neglected, physically abused, sexually abused children, and children whose parents were psychologically unavailable.[10]

As a victim of neglect in childhood, Grace demonstrated some of these effects in her adult life. Before getting help through the Exodus support group ministry, Grace easily began sexual relationships with other women. But she just as easily ended them. Her lack of ability to bond at an intimate, emotional level displayed itself even within her lesbian relationships.

Sexual Abuse

As noted, two-thirds of the women responding to my survey reported being sexually abused. All of those women were molested by men; however, one-quarter of the girls molested by men also reported being molested by women. Here is how the male perpetrators are identified:

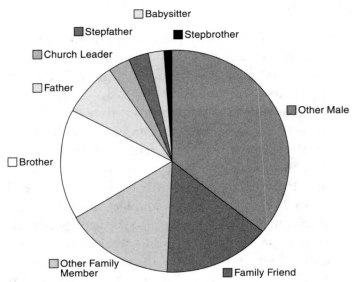

Male Molesters
(66.4% of the women I surveyed were molested by men)

The long-term effects of sexual abuse have been well documented by both researchers and those involved in the health professions. A well-known and long-time researcher in this area is Dr. David Finkelhor of the University of New Hampshire. In his 1990 review of the literature, published in *Professional Psychology: Research and Practice,* Dr. Finkelhor writes,

> Boys, like girls, show marked impact as a result of sexual abuse both early and long term....The studies evaluating children shortly after disclosure show boys with the same patterns of stress-related symptoms as girls: fears, sleep problems, and distractedness....For women, however, the psychopathology associated with abuse history was more extensive, falling in the area of affective disorders (depression, mania), anxiety disorders (phobias, panic, and obsessive-compulsive behavior), and alcohol abuse. Previous studies have shown that sexually abused girls are more likely to suffer sexual revictimization later in life.[11]

Another review states,

> Victims of sexual abuse frequently experience feelings of shame, guilt, isolation, powerlessness, embarrassment, and inadequacy. They may even accept responsibility for the abuse by blaming themselves....Early identification of sexual abuse victims appears crucial to reduction of suffering, enhancement of psychological development, and for healthier adult functioning....As long as disclosure continues to be a problem for young victims, then fear, suffering, and psychological distress will, like the secret, remain with the victim.[12]

Let's consider for a moment the effects on a young girl of sexual molestation by another female. If a girl is molested by an older female, she may naturally question her sexual identity. This may especially be the case if the girl isn't feeling connected to or identifying with her mother, if she has unmet emotional needs for her mother's attention and nurture, or if the psuedo-intimate interaction brought any degree of pleasure. Because she may be desperate for a sense of feeling special and cared for, the young girl may misunderstand the attention she is getting from a female molester as love. A little girl's valid but unmet need to connect with her mother may be transposed into sexual connection with other girls.

Chastity Bono is an example of this dynamic. In her book *The End of Innocence,* Chastity writes about Joan, a lesbian who was a friend of her mother's. She writes:

> My mom wasn't always around, since she was working, so Joan sort of filled in that gap. She always took the time and effort to make me feel loved and appreciated. My mom was career-driven, and for good reason: She had two kids and other family members to support. But at that time I wasn't able to rationalize that my mom was thinking of me and my needs by working: I just focused on the fact that I wasn't getting enough attention, and I often felt lonely or abandoned. When I spent time with Joan, I felt like the center of attention, even when there were a lot of other people around her. She had the gift for making people feel special.[13]

That feeling of being special—if engendered through an inappropriate relationship—will one day be the source of pain for most women who were abused as girls. Let's consider the processes these and other women have used to deal with pain from the past.

Recovering from Abuse

As we've seen, many options for help in dealing with childhood abuse are available, including Christian therapists specializing in grief or specific childhood issues, marriage and family counselors, and support groups.

But beyond these, other tools have proved extremely helpful to many women (and men) dealing with a difficult past.

One such tool is Scripture. Many of us have found great power and solace when reviewing what God says about our identity in the Bible. For example, God says that each of us is beloved by God and kept for Jesus Christ. "Those who are called, beloved in God the Father, and kept for Jesus Christ" (Jude 1 NASB). We're also told in Scripture that we're daughters of the Great King with an inheritance in heaven:

> Also we have obtained an inheritance, having been predestined according to His purpose who works all things after the counsel of His will...In Him, you also, after listening to the message of truth, the gospel of your salvation—having also believed, you were sealed in Him with the Holy Spirit of promise, who is given as a pledge of our inheritance...(Ephesians 1:11,13-14 NASB).

There are hundreds of great promises for those who believe. We have the *ultimate* good Father now. Only God can provide us with the *perfect* and *pure* love that we have always craved and found missing in earthly relationships. He alone has an endless love and affection for us. All other wells will quickly run dry, but not God's. By meditating on Scripture and memorizing some of the great healing verses, we are able to renew our mind...literally *change* our mind about our identity—and our past. Sadly, we too often replay hurtful words and deeds from our past in our mind like a broken tape player. In so doing, we continually reinforce the pain of the past.

Mike Haley, a Christian colleague and friend of mine—and also a former homosexual—wrote down the lies that he believed about himself on one side of index cards and then flipped them over and wrote the truth of Scripture on the other side. Whenever he was starting to believe one of those old lies, he would read the scriptural side of the card.

The concept of renewing our minds is one of God's remedies for overcoming the pain of the past. The Apostle Paul writes, "Do not conform any longer to the pattern of this world, but be transformed by the renewing of your mind. Then you will be able to test and approve what God's will is—his good, pleasing and perfect will" (Romans 12:2).

Recognizing the Pain

Many of us tend to run away from our past. I have heard many preachers say, "Don't look back, just move forward." But that attitude may encourage wounded people to continue to walk in wounded ways. Dealing with your painful past is the beginning of a new start in life. You are the one who can stop some of the dangerous cycles that have wounded you. But first you must recognize your past experiences for what they were—wrong. You should not have had to walk through such painful experiences in childhood, but you did. Other's choices—their action or their inaction—may have been devastating. Jan Frank, author of *A Door of Hope*, writes concerning this step, "The first step of recovery is to face the problem—the infected wound that hasn't healed."[14]

Instead of running from the perfect Surgeon, the Doctor of our souls, we need to hold still so that He can operate! Jesus said, *"It is not the healthy who need a doctor, but the sick. I have not come to call the righteous, but sinners"* (Mark 2:17).

Recounting the Abuse

Recounting our abuse can be a particularly difficult step, so you need to be sure that you are in a safe and confidential environment. Jan Frank encourages, "Talking about the incident doesn't change the event or its impact, but it does release some of the emotion surrounding your experience.... For the victim, it is extremely important that she look in depth at her experience because she has spent a lifetime avoiding the pain."[15]

Allowing Yourself to Experience Feelings

When I first became a Christian and began facing a sexual abuse incident from my early childhood (age four), I began by recounting the incident to my pastoral counselor. At first I didn't particularly feel anything concerning the incident. My emotions seemed frozen and detached—as if I wasn't the one that was injured by the individual. My feelings took a while to connect with that little girl (me) who was so confused at such a young age.

Some people worry that if they allow themselves to feel, they will fall into a bottomless pit of hopelessness or rage. But I have seen again and again that concern give way to the relief that verbally expressing our true feelings with a counselor can bring. "Experiencing feelings is important for anyone who has suffered an emotional hurt," Jan Frank writes. "Unfortunately the Christian community often advises us to ignore, gloss over or put aside our feelings. This can be unwise as our feelings have a way of creeping out anyway, and in ways that can be destructive."[16]

> *You will know the truth, and the truth will set you free (John 8:32).*

Placing Responsibility Where It Belongs

Our desire to protect and maintain unhealthy relationships can impede our ability to place the responsibility for abuse where it really belongs. In fact, this is so common among women clients that a counselor who is an expert in dealing with childhood abuse will probably expect to run into this problem. I am never surprised when I hear it.

Let me give you an example. Maria, a young Hispanic woman, drove an exceptionally long way to attend a support group that several of us led in Marin County, California. After she had been attending for a few months, she began telling us about her anger problems at home. We learned about her relationship with her mother, who had been psychologically ill for most of her life. Whenever her feelings about her mother's poor treatment of her erupted, she would wave the temporary magic wand of dismissal, "Oh, she really couldn't help herself. She was ill."

These comments did nothing to validate the pain Maria had incurred at the hands of her mentally ill mother. Instead, by dismissing her mother's responsibility, Maria left herself with nowhere to go. The message she gave herself repeatedly was to not trust her own intuition, nor to allow herself to feel and work through the pain. So she stalled in the place of pain until she was able to place the responsibility where it belonged. Perhaps the strong family loyalty that exists within the Hispanic community reinforced this thinking as well.

Eventually, Maria broke down and wept during one of our meetings. She was able to allow herself to feel—finally! And that freedom actually came as a result of realizing she was not to blame for the physical and verbal abuse that her mother had unleashed on her from childhood. Her tears of pain were also tears of relief.

My own feelings emerged more fully after I began to examine who was really responsible for my sexual abuse. I had felt dirtied by the experience and assumed I was at least partly responsible even though I was four years old and my abuser was twelve. As I began to think about it in the counseling office, particularly the vulnerability of a four-year-old compared to the strength of a twelve-year-old, I became very angry. I began to feel. After the session, I went out of the office, found a quiet spot, and just cried.

Here's what Jan Frank says about the responsibility of children: "Let me make a very bold, but factual statement. A child victim is 100 percent free of any responsibility. *The aggressor is always fully responsible.*"[17]

Confronting the Abuser

Confrontation with your abuser is not always possible, nor is it always advisable. You should check with your health-care professional before taking this step. If not timed and prepared correctly, it could be emotionally damaging instead of helpful.

One of my friends who was coming out of lesbianism had been molested by her grandfather. Since Leslie was in her mid-thirties and her grandfather had passed away more than a decade earlier, confronting him was impossible. Leslie was traveling home for her mother's birthday. Before she went, she prepared herself to visit his grave and even wrote a note to him about her feelings of pain and confusion.

One afternoon Leslie drove to the cemetery and read her note aloud to the gravestone as if her grandfather were there. Clearly, he was long gone, but the gravestone stood in his place. There, alone before her abuser's grave, Leslie was free to cry and express her feelings. She returned home more resolved and able to move on in her life.

Your counselor may encourage you to write a note or letter to the person who hurt you, but not to send it. Instead, take it to your appointment and read it to the counselor, pretending he or she is the offending person.

As Jan Frank so clearly articulates, "Confrontation... enables the victim to take the burden of responsibility and place it in the rightful hands of the aggressor and any co-contributors."[18]

Forgiving the Offender

Forgiveness is a hallmark of Christianity, of following Jesus. We sin, ask for forgiveness from God, and are freely forgiven—"If we confess our sins, He is faithful and just and will forgive us our sins and purify us from all unrighteousness. If we claim we have not sinned, we make Him out to be a liar and His word has no place in our lives" (1 John 1:9-10). The Lord's Prayer demonstrates our responsibility to pass that forgiveness along to others: "Forgive us our sins, for we also forgive everyone who sins against us" (Luke 11:4). Jesus also explained forgiveness in a parable:

> "Should you not also have had mercy on your fellow slave, even as I had mercy on you?" And his lord, moved with anger, handed him over to the torturers until he should repay all that was owed him. So shall my heavenly Father also do to you, if each of you does not forgive his brother from your heart (Matthew 18:33-35).

Once we have acknowledged who is responsible for our childhood abuse or neglect, and have allowed ourselves to feel the pain of the wound, the next step is to begin the process of forgiveness. Much can be said about what forgiveness is, what it is not, and how to go about it. First of all, forgiveness is something that is unmerited and undeserved. According to *Vine's Expository Dictionary*, to forgive is "to remit or forgive debts, these being completely cancelled" and "to bestow favor unconditionally."[19]

Some women say that they are reluctant to forgive their offenders because they are afraid their forgiveness removes the penalty or responsibility for the offense. But we must understand that we are all guilty of sin, which means to "miss the mark." The Apostle Paul declares, "For all have sinned and fall short of the glory of God" (Romans 3:23). And again, "But God demonstrates his own love for us in this: While we were still sinners, Christ died for us" (Romans 5:8). Peter teaches that God's character is such that He is "patient with you, not wanting anyone to perish, but everyone to come to repentance" (2 Peter 3:9). To receive heavenly forgiveness, the abuser would need to repent, believe, and turn to God to receive forgiveness—just as we all must do. Perhaps God will soften his or her heart to repent or perhaps not. That call is the Lord's, not ours.

If you are unwilling to forgive, my first recommendation is to at least be willing to be willing to forgive. I remember having a hard time with even that simple task! But my prayer for weeks and what seemed like months was, "Lord, I am unwilling to forgive my abuser. But I am willing to be willing." When I was finally able to move to the next step, I offered a legal form of forgiveness. It was very nonemotional, but I was at least able to say the words in prayer, "Lord, I forgive that young man."

What was *much* harder was forgiving this man *from my heart!* I could say the words, but I knew that heartfelt forgiveness was far beyond my own capacity. So once again I prayed seriously, "Lord, you say to forgive from my heart, but I cannot change my heart. Please do this work so that I can obey You in this way too."

It took a while, but I did find that my heart was changing toward my abuser. I began to feel compassion for him and to recognize that I had hurt people in my life too. In fact, I began to understand that I was just as worthy of death and separation from God as he was yet Christ had forgiven me. My heart was moved with true compassion for the first time toward this individual. God had answered my prayer.

After offering true forgiveness to the ones who had hurt me the most, I found great freedom to become the woman of confidence and joy that God had always intended me to be. My obedience and God's provision set me free from the bondage of bitterness and festering anger. And boy, did that feel good!

A Brief Review

Childhood experiences of abuse (or witnessing abuse) can have devastating consequences in a woman's (or man's) life. Far from having merely momentary impact, residual effects can distort perception for the rest of the victim's life if left untreated. Common side effects for women are depression, anxiety, alcohol abuse, and difficulty bonding in intimate relationships with others. Compared with the federal statistics on the rate of abuse, women dealing with same-sex attraction reported much higher rates of abuse in all categories, according to my 2000 study.

But the wounded can find hope in God's Word, in His Church, and through His Spirit (2 Corinthians 1:3, Matthew 5:4, and Isaiah 61:1-3). In contrast to the pain of the past, God's Word offers us acceptance, love, and new identity. He alone can break the power of the negative words and experiences of the past and give us a hope and a future.

"For I know the plans I have for you," declares the LORD,
    "plans to prosper you and not to harm you,
plans to give you a hope and a future" (Jeremiah 29:11).

7

Overcoming Temptation

"*I* am a 30-year-old single woman, and before I came to know Christ a few years ago...I had three romantic relationships with female friends," one woman wrote on Crosswalk.com. "But in the years since then," she continued, "whenever I get close to a female friend, I will feel the temptations and I need to constantly restrain my emotions toward them (it has happened with four women so far) because I know it is wrong."[1]

Let us then approach the throne of grace with confidence, so that we may receive mercy and find grace to help us in our time of need (Hebrews 4:16).

Some strategies for overcoming temptation are more effective than others. Simple restraint doesn't go very far in dealing with same-sex attractions. In fact, very few are able to overcome any form of temptation by willpower alone. So I wasn't surprised to read the woman's next sentence: "But now I have succumbed to temptation with one of these women." I was surprised she maintained the first three relationships without engaging in lesbian sex.

She continued in her next post, writing about becoming a Christian just a few years before, "I made a promise to myself that I want to live a Spirit-filled life, righteous and free from

> The grass is always greener, where you water it (Erma Bombeck).

sin. I claimed the promise of 2 Corinthians 5:17, "Therefore, if anyone is in Christ, he is a new creation; the old has gone, the new has come." I was so thrilled to learn about this and I told myself that I would never engage in lesbianism again." She asserted that now she would surely have the strength and power to "deter all [lesbian] thoughts and temptations whenever they appear."[2]

Unfortunately, this woman had a couple of unhelpful assumptions. First, when she came to Christ, she seemed to believe that Christian willpower would be enough to fight off temptations. Second, she thought that perhaps the attractions she had toward women before becoming a Christian would vanish completely. Sadly, the woman will probably not succeed in her quest to live a "Spirit-filled life, righteous and free from sin" unless she investigates the reasons why she is drawn so powerfully to other women. She would also surely benefit from knowing a few more practical, biblical tools for overcoming temptation.

On the next few pages, we'll look at the process of temptation and explore some practical ways to deal with it. Encouragement is my main objective. You are not alone. Your temptation is not unique. Others before you have succeeded. Some have failed at times and yet moved on to find wholeness in Christ.

Jane's Story

"When I was five, I accepted Christ into my heart. I worshiped God, attended church, and now have been married for almost 25 years," Jane Boyer shared at Focus on the Family's Love Won Out conference. "But for a good part of my marriage, I lived a double life. One as a Christian and one as a homosexual....I was filled with guilt, shame, and self-hatred."[3]

Jane talked about her family background as well. "My father was a violent and abusive man, and I developed an intense hatred in my heart for men....My mother was emotionally unavailable to meet my needs as a child because she was a victim of my father's violence.

"I was her caretaker, her protector, and felt resentful of her because I perceived her as very weak, ineffective, and passive....If being a woman meant being a victim—helpless, vulnerable to abuse, used as a sex object by men—I didn't want any part of it."

Looking back, Jane said, "my needs for love and acceptance were not being met at home." So when she was just 13 years old, she turned to alcohol and drugs, "to ease and numb the pain and loneliness." Later, she married and soon after was introduced to gay bars, and her double life began.

When talking about the gay bars, Jane explained what drew her so powerfully. "I belonged and felt accepted because I came from a background of rejection, so acceptance was something I wanted, whatever the cost."

Regarding temptation and her attempts to break away from the gay bar scene, Jane said, "Time and time again, I would vow I would never return to the gay bar, only to go back again and again...The pull for love and acceptance was too powerful. As time went on, I began to see my gay friends were also in deep emotional pain from their pasts and many were in conflict over their homosexual feelings...We were all looking for that perfect love and perfect relationship and never seemed to find it."

Temptation Versus Sin

Temptation is an offer to resolve our needs or wants in a way that is in opposition to God's expressed will. For example, if I consider betraying a personal confidence as a solution to feeling disconnected from others at church or in a social setting, I am being tempted. Gossip is against God's expressed will (Proverbs 11:13, 2 Corinthians 12:20). Likewise, a thought of a previous sexual relationship is an offer to escape daily frustrations or pressures. It is temptation.

But temptation is not sin. Sin, by contrast, is taking up the offer. Sin occurs when we act in willful defiance of God's law and character. We no longer sit back as passive observers; instead, we become participants.

How does the transition happen between temptation and sin? A process of consent occurs in our hearts. For some of us, the process happens very rapidly, and we don't see that a decision has even occurred. Others of us may be well versed in not acting on an errant thought but still may be unaware of the steps that occur between temptation and sin.

We must remember that temptation is not judged in the Bible; rather, sin is. In fact, even the Lord Jesus Christ encountered temptation. The most obvious example occurred after Jesus was baptized by John in the Jordan river and "was led by the Spirit into the desert to be tempted by the devil" (Matthew 4:1). The writer of Hebrews declared,

> Therefore, since we have a great high priest who has gone through the heavens, Jesus the Son of God, let us hold firmly to the faith we profess. For we do not have a high priest who is unable to sympathize with our weaknesses, but we have one who has been tempted in every way, just as we are—yet was without sin (Hebrews 4:14-15).

Qualities of Temptation

Over the course of more than 20 years of ex-gay and other Christian ministry, I have noticed some common qualities of temptation. Temptation often promises to immediately resolve our needs or wants. In other words, temptation is sometimes an inappropriate shortcut; it offers us the opportunity to take control ourselves rather than wait for God's answer and provision for our needs. Sin is a counterfeit solution to our needs. No waiting. No need for exercising self-control. Just immediate action—and then guilt and shame.

The Bible promises that we will encounter trials and temptation. "Dear friends, do not be surprised at the painful trial you are suffering, as though something strange were happening to you"(1 Peter 4:12). Your personal form of temptation is not unique. In fact, the Bible declares it "common to man [meaning male and female]" (1 Corinthians 10:13).

The Cycle of Temptation and Sin

Let's take a more in-depth look at the cycle of temptation and sin. As mentioned, the cycle often begins with an unresolved need or want. So step one is a *yearning for fulfillment* in some area of our lives. We all desire meaningful relationships, a fulfilling purpose, and hope for the future. We may feel frustration on the job or elsewhere, practice unforgiveness, lack an attitude of gratitude, or simply wrestle with the day-to-day changes in life.

I recently spoke with a woman who was experiencing all sorts of wonderful changes in her life and career, but those changes left her feeling vulnerable to lesbian temptation. Sydney, a 20-something woman told me, "I was craving a secure connection with another woman that would seem to tell me that everything would turn out all right." Her unresolved needs were security and stability.

Step two is *enticement*. We must remember that another power is at work in our universe, someone who wants to rob us. Jesus said, "The thief comes only to steal and kill and destroy"(John 10:10). The devil is also called "the tempter" (1 Thessalonians 3:5). His main ploys are enticement, discouragement, and intimidation because once we become Christians, we actually have much greater power than Satan does. This is only because, as the apostle John wrote, "The one who is in you is greater than the one who is in the world" (1 John 4:4).

Let's consider Sydney's enticement. She longed for security and stability at a time in her life that was filled with change. The counterfeit solution was a sexual connection with another woman. Would that have solved her problem of feeling insecure and disconnected? Only in an incomplete and temporary manner. Her sexual relationship with another woman would have made her feel "cut off" from her relationship with God.

This disconnect with God is important to note. It occurred not only in my own life in 1986 but also in the lives of many other women attempting to overcome same-sex attraction. In fact, the women who participated in my survey sought freedom from lesbianism because of their "relationship with God" (95 percent reported this reason).[4]

Enticement finds a weakness in us because we still have a sinful nature. This is what James has to say: "When tempted, no one should say, 'God is tempting me.' For God cannot be tempted by evil, nor does he tempt anyone; but each one is tempted when, by his own evil desire, he is dragged away and enticed" (James 1:13-14). Enticement also implies some appeal to us. *Vine's Expository Dictionary* defines *entice* as primarily "To lure by a bait."[5] A seductive element appeals to our lower nature and makes us want to follow the bait.

The third step of the temptation/sin cycle is a *mental preoccupation* with the bait. In the book *Every Man's Battle* by Stephen Arterburn, Fred Stoeker, and Mike Yorkey, the writers instruct men struggling for sexual purity to develop an outer perimeter with their eyes. "Think of the first perimeter (your eyes) as your outermost defense, a wall with 'Keep Out' signs around it. It defends your eyes by covenant (as Job did: 'I made a covenant with my eyes not to look lustfully at a girl'), and you do that by training your eyes to *bounce* from objects of lust."[6] The first glance is free; the second look is not. The same goes for women dealing with same-sex attraction. The fact that you're tempted shouldn't worry you, but you must decide what to do with the temptation.

In 1993, I was asked by Oprah Winfrey on her talk show if I still encounter homosexual thoughts. I answered, "Yes, but the intensity has lessened. It is almost like swatting a fly off of my shoulder." The problem is not the temptation but our dwelling on the temptation. We can easily stop the cycle at this step. Stopping it later becomes much more difficult.

Let me use another example from my life. This incident had nothing to do with same-sex attraction, but I encountered temptation nonetheless. I was shopping, and my one-year-old son had picked up a package of batteries at the checkout counter without my knowledge. The grocery store clerk didn't see him either, and I pushed my cart of groceries outside without paying for the batteries.

Once outside, I realized what had happened and hesitated for just a moment. One thought came to me: "You spend so much money here—just take them." But I dismissed that thought and walked back into the store. I explained to the customer service employee what had happened and gave her the unpaid-for batteries. You should have seen the surprised look on her face!

Instead of taking the bait, I refused to be led by an errant thought of stealing. Then I took action to make the situation right. Returning the batteries would have been much harder to do if I had knowingly driven away with them. I would have had to turn around not only my car but also my will. I could have accepted the justification of stealing: "they owe it to me." I share this example because sometimes we can more easily see the steps of temptation in an area other than sexual temptation.

In step four we *plan, strategize, and deliberately partner with temptation.* This is also where sin begins. Perhaps you have heard the quip, "You can't prevent birds from flying over your head, but you can prevent them from building a nest in your hair." Fantasy and preoccupation invites temptation to nest.

Step five is *engaging in the sinful action itself.* We are no longer in the fantasy or planning stage—we are *there.* And it may feel good, but just for a moment. Satisfaction is fleeting. "By faith Moses, when he had grown up, refused to be called the son of Pharaoh's daughter; choosing rather to endure ill-treatment with the people of God, than to enjoy the passing pleasure of sin" (Hebrews 11:24-25, NASB). Anyone who has indulged in sin can recognize that its pleasure is indeed "passing."

The ironic aspect of sin is found in step six, *condemnation.* The very one who was enticing and baiting now stands to condemn us. Not only is Satan called "the tempter," but he is also called "the accuser" (Revelation 12:10, NASB). Now that the table is turned, we deal with a list of negative emotions such as guilt, shame, condemnation, and remorse. And sin "picks our pocket" of what we possessed before the cycle kicked in—confidence, peace with God, joy, truly solid rela-tionships, integrity, self-respect, respect from others, sound mind, and power and authority, just to name a few. We can also believe the lie that we cannot possibly go to God with our troubles now. Don't we have to clean up our act first?

Spiritual bankruptcy can drive us to the sin cycle all over again. Thankfully, however, we have another solution! Either sin deceives us all over again (Hebrews 3:13) or we can run to Him who can cleanse us from all sin. If we choose to run away from God, we will eventually run back to sin. And should we choose to sin again and again, we will encounter more spiritual bondage. Sin always requires more sin and deeper forms of depravity to get the same temporary relief. The downward spiral continues.

Morgan, a woman from California in her mid-40s, recently told me about her journey. "In my 20s, I started my lesbian involvement by looking for that one incredible woman that I could commit my life to. But after five years, found myself floating from relationship to relationship. In the bars, I was never able to keep my eyes from wandering to the next potential partner—even when I was 'with' someone else." Her story illustrates Paul's words:

> Don't you know that when you offer yourselves to someone to obey him as slaves, you are slaves to the one whom you obey—whether you are slaves to sin, which leads to death, or to obedience, which leads to righteousness?... Just as you used to offer the parts of your body in slavery to impurity and to ever-increasing wickedness, so now offer them in slavery to righteousness leading to holiness (Romans 6:16,19).

Hope for the Hurting Heart

So what if we find ourselves in the cycle of sin or have invested in sin? We have great hope because God knows how to deal with sin! This is one reason why I knew that God would change my heart in the area of same-sex attraction. If homosexuality is sin, then God most certainly has both the plan and resources to save us from sin!

The apostle Paul wrote concerning himself and the dynamic of sin, "What a wretched man I am! Who will rescue me from this body of death? Thanks be to God—through Jesus Christ our Lord!" (Romans 7:24-25). How wonderful! Jesus died to free us from slavery to sin. And, what's more, He encourages us to "approach the throne of grace with confidence, so that we may receive mercy and find grace to help us in our time of need" (Hebrews 4:16).

Instead of running away from God, we can run *to* God just as we are! Another one of my favorite verses is 1 John 1:9—

"If we confess our sins, he is faithful and just and will forgive us our sins and purify us from all unrighteousness."

Does that mean that we can just keep on sinning and asking forgiveness without submitting ourselves to God's will? Paul gracefully addresses all of these thoughts and concerns in great depth in his letter to the Romans, specifically chapters 6 through 8. In chapter 6 he writes, "Are we to continue in sin that grace might increase? May it never be! How shall we who died to sin still live in it?" (Romans 6:1-2, NASB). And again, in chapter 8, "If you are living according to the flesh [that is, the sinful nature], you must die; but if by the Spirit you are putting to death the deeds of the body [again, the sinful nature], you will live. For all who are being led by the Spirit of God, these are the sons of God"(Romans 8:13-14, NASB).

The devil uses temptation to cause us to falter and fail, but God allows us to be tested in order to prove our faith and mold our character. He also desires for us to master temptation (Genesis 4:6-7, James 1:2-4, 1 Peter 1:6-9).

> Blessed is the man who perseveres under trial, because when he has stood the test, he will receive the crown of life that God has promised to those who love him (James 1:12).

Practical Help When Dealing with Temptation

"Okay," you say, "I understand the difference between temptation and sin, the cycle of temptation and sin, the fact that I can approach God, and that though Satan intends evil, God tests us in order to approve us. Great! But how do I succeed in overcoming the almost daily temptation in my female relationships, fantasy life, or the solitary struggle of various forms of pornography and sexual addiction?"

What an excellent question! My hope is that this section will guide you through some practical guidelines that can help you win your battles.

Accountability

As I mentioned in chapter 5, establishing a support system and sharing with someone else can make a big difference. Choose wisely whom you share with. If you really want to win the battle before you, you should choose individuals who can encourage you with your goals. For example, I would not recommend looking to someone else currently in the gay lifestyle for personal support.

Instead, God's design for His church is to "confess your sins to each other and pray for each other so that you may be healed. The prayer of a righteous man is powerful and effective" (James 5:16). Asking our brothers and sisters in Christ to pray for us is a powerful way to bring our struggles into the light as opposed to staying in private, silent bondage to our sinful patterns. This, of course, needs to take place with trusted and mature Christians. Another good idea is to give them permission to ask you, "How is it going with what you shared with me?"

Look Beyond the Temptation

Sometimes we can focus too intently on our temptations. Instead, we need to understand what our truest, deepest desires really are and then to seek to meet them in godly ways.

Let's return for a moment to Sydney. Her deep needs were for emotional security and stability as she walked through the exciting changes happening in her life. She later remarked,

> I used to think that struggling with homosexuality was the single most difficult thing in the world to

overcome. Not only did I feel perfectly unsafe talking about it with anyone, I was also keenly aware of the stigma attached to the issue of same-sex attractions. I was fully convinced that there was nothing more painful than longing for something that seemed as natural as breathing, yet knowing the fulfillment of these desires through homosexuality would be in direct opposition to the heart of God. I was certain that no one else struggled like I did.

When she began sharing her struggles with a female Christian counselor, Sydney began to realize how the counselor's previous struggle of inappropriate desires toward a married man paralleled her own temptations. Sydney explained,

She understood from a very personal and empathetic level everything with which I was dealing, though she had never struggled with homosexuality. I used to get so hung up on the same-sex attraction element when really what was at the core of my sin had little to do with sex. It has become abundantly evident to me that many women are seeking to find their sufficiency in someone or something else, other than God. I am not alone.

Take a moment and consider a few questions you may want to ask yourself. They may help you pinpoint why you are vulnerable to temptation.

- What stresses am I dealing with in my life?

- What, if anything, is changing in my world?

- What emotions are being stirred? Loneliness? Boredom? Fear or apprehension? Sadness? Anger? Loss of control?

- Am I focusing on one female relationship to meet my needs?

- Am I progressing too quickly in my friendship with another woman? Can I see her faults as well as her gifts and abilities?

Sometimes underlying thoughts that motivate us are hidden quite deep below the surface and are not obvious. For instance, if I feel like I'm not worth relating to, I may cling too tightly to someone who seems to contradict that inward belief. If I am finally beginning to look at painful memories from my past, the desire to emotionally distract myself from the pain or the fear of pain, may be my motivator to try to connect with another woman sexually or through fantasy. In short, we are complex creatures with many more thoughts and feelings than we probably recognize. To see our true motivations, we need to look way beyond the temptation itself to what's going on emotionally within us.

Then we should ask ourselves, *Would sex with that woman to whom I am attracted right now solve the real need that I'm facing?* The answer is clearly no. So be honest about your real feelings with those that care about you, and seek to express those feelings in ways that please God. If you are discouraged or lonely or feeling insecure, share your feelings with someone you trust. Your mentor, counselor, pastor, or friend can then help you find ways to properly address your true needs. These feelings happen to them as well but may make them vulnerable to a different form of temptation. Just as Sydney discovered, you truly have much more in common with others than you know!

Specific Boundaries

No matter how intense your feelings may be, I cannot emphasize this first principle enough: *Do not share your attraction with the woman to whom you are attracted.* The one exception is that you might share your attraction with your counselor, who is not a friend and who sees you within certain preset time parameters.

"Why shouldn't I share my attraction with her?" you might ask. "Although she is a friend, she isn't from a homosexual background."

Following this principle is important for many reasons. First, I am assuming that you wish to overcome same-sex attraction. You are responsible to make "no provision for the flesh [sinful nature] in regard to its lusts" (Romans 13:14, NASB). By telling her of your attraction, you are forging the possibility of a sexual relationship with her. You just never know what she is going through in her life—difficulty in marriage, parenting problems, personal disappointments, the need to feel special to someone...and the list goes on.

Another reason is that attractions come and go. Our feelings will die down as we get to know the person. A good way to pray is, *Lord help me to see her as you see her.* Our emotions can settle as we get to know the true and independent person whom we admire.

Lastly, if we tell another woman of our attraction to her, we move from dealing with our feelings safely and moving past the attraction, to the possibility of rejection. The "object of your affection" may treat you differently and distantly from then on, or perhaps she may pull back completely.

Within specific boundaries, healthy female relationships can thrive for the woman coming out of lesbianism, and those will be more fully discussed in chapter 8.

Avoid places that can lead directly to sin: lesbian or gay bookstores, parties, bars, and other such places. You alone know what other weak spots you have. You can always let your mentor, counselor, or other accountability partner know where you need help and have them ask you about it.

Also avoid drugs and alcohol, which impair your thinking when dealing with temptation. And don't be alone with someone to whom you're attracted after midnight. As Mike Haley, Gender and Youth Analyst at Focus on the Family, often says, "Nothing good ever happens after midnight!"

Be Proactive in Renewing Your Mind

Renewing our minds, discussed in the previous chapter, is a simple concept but can be quite challenging to apply as we overcome temptation. Scripture tells us to "take captive every thought to make it obedient to Christ" (2 Corinthians 10:5). And again, "whatever is true, whatever is noble, whatever is right, whatever is pure, whatever is lovely, whatever is admirable—if anything is excellent or praiseworthy—think about such things" (Philippians 4:8).

This applies working your way out of a current partnership, flashbacks to old relationships, and any mental imagery you may deal with. When an uninvited thought comes to mind, you must decide what to do with it.

When I was first coming out of lesbian relationships, I remember the surges of feelings that would accompany any reminder of my "ex." Our minds have the capacity to play back scenes triggered by sounds, scents, women of similar physical appearance, and other such things. But we have the ability to redirect our thinking. The less we dwell on those memories, the more power over them we will have. They will grow weaker, and we will grow stronger.

But how do we practice this principle? First, we fill our mind with what is good, lovely, admirable, pure, and true while we're *not* facing temptation. Memorizing Scripture is the best way to do this. It fills our minds with God's words and will help in our time of temptation.

Second, when the uninvited thoughts get stirred up, redirect them to anything worth your attention. When I had just begun my journey out of a lesbian relationship and had the help of an Exodus International ministry, feelings would frequently overtake me for the first few months. All of a sudden, a flashback to a sexually intimate moment would occur out of the blue. In my determination to not dwell on the thought, I would try to distract myself, maybe by looking out the window and speaking to myself out loud, "What a beautiful tree over there...the colors of those leaves are just gorgeous." Yes, it sounds kind of silly, I admit—but for me, it worked. I had no idea at the time that I was renewing my mind. That mental practice gave me a skill that would prove to be very useful!

Also, remember that flashbacks to old relationships never offer clear reality. Instead Satan offers us the best of yesterday or a perfect illusion. At the time of temptation, the deceiver will not remind us of conflicts that we had in that relationship, bad breath, smelly feet, or a sense of loneliness we had while in the relationship. These things would ruin temptation's appeal. He knows very well that illusion is more appealing than reality. As the writers share in *Every Man's Battle*, "Facts are the killer virus of attractions."[7]

Battling Spiritually in Prayer

Other powerful principles will also prove useful in overcoming temptation. For as the apostle Paul wrote to the Corinthian church, "The weapons we fight with are not the weapons of the world. On the contrary, they have divine power to demolish strongholds. We demolish arguments and every pretension that sets itself up against the knowledge of God" (2 Corinthians 10:4-5). So here are some compelling ideas for use in prayer, particularly useful in a gathering of at least two other female prayer warriors.

■ Verbally renounce your slavery to sin, and accept your new role as a "temple of the Lord" (Romans 6:19, 1 Corinthians 3:16).

■ Allow yourself to grieve the loss of an ex-partner or emotionally exclusive relationship. When we give up a sinful relationship, we also experience the loss of what was good about the relationship.

■ Break same-flesh unions or spiritual soul ties in prayer. Ask the Lord to sever any remaining unhealthy link to the person in the spiritual realm. Yield the past relationships to the Lord and then pray a blessing upon each individual. The Bible teaches that when sexual activity occurs, a spiritual link is formed between individuals (1 Corinthians 6:15-20).

■ Ask God to give you His perspective on what enchants your sinful nature. We often have a double mind as we begin to pursue change. On one hand, we are ashamed and long for intimacy with God. On the other the struggle shows that we love our sin. In other words, ask God to give you a hatred for *your* sin and also an undivided heart (Psalm 86:11; Jeremiah 17:7-14; Ezekiel 11:19).

A silly idea is current that good people do not know what temptation means. This is an obvious lie. Only those who try to resist temptation know how strong it is....A man who gives in to temptation after five minutes simply does not know what it would have been like an hour later....We never find out the strength of the evil impulse inside us until we try to fight it: and Christ, because He was the only man who never yielded to temptation, is the only man who knows to the full what temptation means—the only complete realist (C.S. Lewis).[8]

Dealing with Sexual Fantasy or Addiction

In addition to the normal day-to-day temptation common to same-sex attraction, we must also know how to deal with sexually addictive behavior. Not all women face this issue, but many do deal with different elements of addictive behavior. Of the 265 women in my survey, more than 90 percent dealt with same-sex fantasy in the form of personal imagination. And almost 60 percent had viewed movies that involved same-sex fantasy. Almost half had used visual pornography; 20 percent had sought lesbian porn on the Internet. And one-third of the women had engaged in same-sex fantasy through the medium of lesbian novels or romances.[9]

Needless to say, sexual fantasy and addiction are problems women who struggle with lesbianism must face. In our Internet age, coming generations of women and men may be hooked more deeply and at a younger age. Current research seems to indicate that "cybersex" is fueling more compulsive and addictive sexual behavior. Psychologists at both Stanford and Duquesne universities published a study in the journal, *Sexual Addiction and Compulsivity,* confirming that this is a "hidden public health hazard exploding."[10]

Fantasy and Sexual Addiction

Fantasy could be defined as "desire unhindered by reality." Addiction is defined by Dr. Maressa Hecht Orzack, a Harvard University psychologist, as "When you can't stop, you can't get away from it, and you need to do it more and more often. It's craving it when it's not there. It's being depressed, irritable, or angry" when you cannot get access to what you are addicted to.[11]

Fantasy and addiction have much in common. Sexual fantasy and addiction both are substitutes for genuine intimacy. Stephen Watters, in his book *Real Solutions for Overcoming Internet Addictions,* wrote, "The temptation everyone faces, however, is the desire to take a shortcut—to settle for what [one well-known author] calls 'false intimacy.' Instead of going through the effort required for real intimacy, people often settle for an illusion—an airbrushed image, a virtual reality, a cyberaffair—something that seems to give a high without hurt, ecstasy without expectations, fulfillment without faults."[12]

The Power of Our Imagination

By far, our own imagination is the easiest and most readily available form of same-sex fantasy. It is also, without a doubt, the most difficult to avoid. We may stay away from lesbian movies, magazines, novels, and even avoid using the Internet at home, but we carry our minds with us everywhere.

One woman began attending our Exodus support group not because she had engaged in a sexual relationship with another woman but because of her well-developed fantasy life. She had been nurturing sexual fantasies in her mind for years and eventually went to the library to check out a lesbian book that would take her thoughts to the next level. Her hidden visits to the library became more regular and more difficult to hide because of her responsibilities as a wife and mother of four children. Instead of being emotionally present for her family, she became more reclusive and emotionally detached.

Perhaps you're thinking, *Well, it couldn't have been that bad. After all, it was just her imagination!* In fact, regardless of the substance or method, addiction can have devastating effects on our lives and those who love us.

Neurologically speaking, fantasy can become a well-worn path. Just think about any other repetitive action that you take in your day. For example, consider driving your car to work or the store. At first, when you moved into your home,

You have heard that it was said, "Do not commit adultery." But I tell you that anyone who looks at a woman lustfully has already committed adultery with her in his heart (Matthew 5:27-28).

you took time to learn where everything was. Three months or three years later, you may drive the same route basically on "autopilot." The same goes for sexual fantasy. At first, it takes work to make the fantasy occur, but sexual arousal sends a flood of adrenaline and endorphins to your brain that embeds the memory securely. In the context of marriage, this process reinforces marital intimacy and attraction. Yet apart from the God-ordained relationship between husband and wife, fantasy and sexual arousal builds a well-worn highway that is difficult to eradicate from our minds.

Ted Roberts wrote in his book *Pure Desire,*

> When I am into a good book, I always read with a highlighter pen in hand so I can find the critical information quickly in the future. Similarly, our brains chemically highlight certain events for instant referral, separating the significant from the insignificant. A major aspect of sexual activity is a strong release of adrenaline and endorphins, which is why sexual events become imprinted in the brain.[13]

Are you exercising your mind? What are you thinking about? Are you developing a running mental novel, or are you thinking on whatever is true, noble, right, and pure? Unchecked, same-sex fantasy in your imagination will lead to other forms of fantasy and addiction. That is the natural chain of events.

Masturbation and Fantasy

Although I have found no specific mention of masturbation in Scripture, we are clearly not to fantasize about others. Women's bodies were designed to have a heightened libido during the time of the month when we are ovulating. In marriage and during childbearing years, this natural cycle of a woman's body makes it easier to conceive a child. If we are single, that can be a difficult time of the month for us, even if masturbation is not a common practice in our lives.

In the process of seeking help, several women have entrusted me with their confidence in the matter of masturbation. Instead of merely dealing with the monthly menstrual cycle's hormones, these women struggled with compulsive masturbation—sometimes daily, sometimes several times a day. One woman shared with me that she acted out more if she was bored or disappointed. The traditional addiction HALT theme fit her behavior perfectly: Hungry, Angry, Lonely, or Tired triggering her compulsion.

Lesbian Pornography and Internet Cybersex

If fantasy in our minds is not dealt with, it can lead to renting sexual videos, connecting with pornography online, or otherwise supplementing our own personal fantasies with someone else's. This fuels sexual addiction to pornography. More and more steps are usually required to attain the same erotic response.

"The internet is revolutionizing sexuality," said Al Cooper, clinical director of a sexuality clinic in San Jose, California. He told psychologists that cybersex is changing the definition of sexual compulsion "like crack cocaine changed the field of substance abuse."[14]

Here are a couple of questions to consider:

- How entrenched are you in using the materials?

■ Have you noticed the need for more sexual content to get the same fix? Have you moved from soft porn to more hard-core materials?

Pornography, whether in the form of magazines, books, or the Internet, usually appeals more easily to women who want to keep their distance from true intimacy and real relationships, including perhaps women who are struggling with desires but do not want to live a double life. Pornography may also entice deaf strugglers because of the inherent communication challenges in interpersonal relationships.

Lesbian Novels and Chat Rooms

Romance novels in grocery stores have long been aimed at women readers looking for a romantic getaway from the boring aspects of life. The volume of romance novel sales to women must be astounding. There always seems to be a female-oriented romance novel on the bestsellers list.

Lesbian novels and creative writing tend to be very sexual in content and focus on the erotic relationship between partners. Lesbian authors are using the same appeal as heterosexual romance novels but are more graphic in content and aim for the same-sex attracted woman. Remember, the basis of whole female sexuality is rooted in relationship. That is how we were designed. Romance novels fueling a sense of relationship with a fictitious illusion appeal to a warped sense of our femaleness.

Contrast that with the behavior of some gay men engaging in anonymous sexual encounters with other males in a park, mall bathroom, or bathhouse without even knowing the others' names. I would speculate that most women would not even consider this form of sexual expression—even in the throes of addiction. No, bathhouses and lesbian sex clubs are still the minority of lesbian experience because of the remnant of our original design for relationship.

Steps to Overcoming Sexual Addiction

To experience freedom from addiction, we must *face the truth* and admit to ourselves that we are sexually addicted. This is the first brave step on the road to sexual health. Telling ourselves the truth is powerful and requires action. It's also humbling. For this reason, an important prerequisite is, as Stephen Arterburn and Fred Stoeker write, "You've decided that the slavery of your sexual sin isn't worth your love of sexual sin."[15]

Second, we must *tell someone else* whom we trust. Confession, not silence, can break the cycle. When we share with another person, we should use clinical language (breast versus boob) and not go into graphic detail of what we have experienced. Our goal should be to get help and not give someone else a mental image to deal with later! Silence and privacy maintain the addiction, so confession and sharing is a very important step in overcoming sexual addiction.

Third, with the help of a good Christian addictions counselor, you must *begin the process of recognizing your patterns of addiction and breaking them*. At first, this can be as difficult as stopping a powerful locomotive. But change comes easier with practice and small successes here and there. You will learn through this pattern that your addiction can be mastered. Asking God to show you stopping points through your cycle can be very helpful. Pray and watch for the emotions or circumstances that trigger the beginning of the process. Ask for the power to resist—and celebrate your successes. At first, you may have trouble recognizing the steps that lead you to acting on your addictive behavior, but over time you will readily notice the progressive steps in your thinking.

Recognize the underlying causes of your addiction. For example, are you avoiding an uncomfortable reality, fearing rejection in your relationships, or coping with the unresolved pain of your past through sexual addiction? Stephen Watters states that "sexual addictions are often tied to sexual abuse.

Dr. Patrick Carnes estimates that more than 80 percent of sex addicts were sexually abused at some point in their lives." Marnie Ferree, a counselor in the area of female sex addictions, points out that "female sex addiction often [is] tied to intimacy disorders fueled by lack of nurture, as well as sexual abuse and trauma from past and present relationships."[16]

Finally, if you have tried everything consistently for at least a year and routinely continue to fall into the same traps and behaviors, you may wish to consider asking for mature Christians to dedicate themselves to a certain time and place to pray with you. All involved should prepare with fasting and prayer (unless there is a physical condition limiting them from this). Arrive expecting God to deliver supernatural help, rather than expecting those praying to have the answers.

During the prayer session, verbally give up your right to the behavior (2 Corinthians 4:2) and offer your concerns to the Lord. Then wait and listen. Finally, ask God to remove the power of the obstacle and to bless you in ways only He can.

After a prayer session somewhat like this, a friend of mine emerged with newfound freedom. "I never knew I had a choice before. It's as if a light bulb went on. Now temptation may not be completely gone, but I know that the power to choose is given back to me!"

The heart is deceitful above all things and beyond cure. Who can understand it? Heal me, O LORD, and I will be healed; save me and I will be saved, for you are the one I praise (Jeremiah 17:9,14).

A Final Word of Encouragement

Stephen Watters articulates well why we should engage ourselves with others and not disengage into fantasy and addiction. "The escape, the high, the sense of control, the numbing effect— whatever it is that you've found yourself chasing—is robbing you of a great experience. But it's not just robbing you of real joy; it's robbing you of the joy that can follow pain. The best experiences in life involve overcoming challenges, resolving conflict, exerting effort, and making sacrifices. Addictions pull you away from pain and sacrifice—they encourage you to take the path of least resistance. The payoff is in overcoming the problem, not in bypassing it."[17]

8

$\mathcal{H}$ealthy $\mathcal{F}$emale $\mathcal{F}$riendships

Craving for Intimacy

From infancy to adulthood, women need connection with others to feel fulfilled. Ideally, a sense of healthy intimacy is first established in a girl's relationship with her mother, then her father, siblings, extended family members, and finally her friends. From solid and affirming relationships, she gains a feeling of her own worth and competence and the sense that others can be trusted.

Many of us, however, missed out on these foundational elements in our early years. If this is the case in your life, I encourage you to persevere and fight to gain back what was lost early on. God Himself can rebuild that foundation in our lives, but we cannot passively sit back and expect to be handed the golden relationships and skills that we so long for. Instead, we need to actively pursue health and wholeness.

The solid commitment between faithful friends is established by thousands of seemingly insignificant commitments over the long haul (Drs. Les & Leslie Parrott).[1]

Mike Haley shared during a general session at the 2002 Exodus International conference that one of the five characteristics of individuals who are successful in overcoming homosexuality is that their actions are different from those who abandon the change process.[2] He elaborated by saying, "These individuals make every effort to obey Christ," referencing 2 Peter 1:5-9. He also quoted Jeff Konrad, author of *You Don't Have to Be Gay:* "These people are proactive and not reactive."

Regardless of our sexual struggles, our sense of security derived from early childhood (or our lack of it) can impact our ability to confidently relate to authority and to every person we meet. Dr. Brenda Hunter, a psychologist for women with Minirth-Meier New Life Clinic explains in her book entitled, *In the Company of Women,*

> Finally, I need to say at the outset of our journey together that I have not always felt comfortable in the company of women. Though Granny taught me that intimacy was possible, my mother taught me that intimacy hurt. For Mother, herself a motherless child, intimacy equaled loss and abandonment—a legacy she bequeathed to me. It was only in my forties that I dealt with this early and powerful relationship. And, after much hard work and no little healing, I have come to my present place in life where I am rich in friends, emotionally close to my husband and my daughters, and at peace with my mother and myself. As I have grown more self-accepting, I have come to appreciate the great gifts women give each other. My friend Heidi Brennan summed it up when she said, "To like your sex, you have to like yourself."[3]

Embracing what your mother did have to offer you is a key to overcoming as well. She may well have nurtured you inadequately, but healing comes from identifying with how she was able to love you. If a common trait of women dealing with same-sex attraction, as mentioned in chapter 3, is to disconnect with their mothers, then a route of healing is to forgive her and embrace what she *was* able to give.

Women dealing with same-sex attraction are not the only ones who face this challenge. Many others have encountered this same process in their journey to wholeness as women. Dr. Hunter shares the process she went through: "And, as I discovered when I worked through my own mother yearning, once we go beyond our own resentment and embrace the good our mother gave us, we feel better about ourselves and our sex."[4]

For many of us dealing with same-sex attraction, we have needed to connect with other women intimately, but at times the closeness that we begin to experience as adults can become confused with sexual feelings. Some women have chosen to avoid relationships with other women in order to prevent sexual feelings from emerging. Sadly, this not only isolates, but also creates a well of need that may eventually draw us back into lesbian intimacy.

Instead, if we embrace female friendships and find our place in the larger community of women—church, work, social interests, and interacting with the culture we live in—we will find greater commonality with other women than we ever expected. Feeling secure and content to be "just another woman" will itself resolve much of our same-sex attraction. Women will become demystified and also delightful in a newfound way. Then we will be given new eyes to see delight in female friendships, as authors Dee Brestin and Brenda Hunter share in their books about godly female friendships.

Road Blocks to Healthy Intimacy with Women

When, in my survey, I asked the same-sex attracted women to identify the most challenging aspects of overcoming lesbianism, a majority answered loneliness. The next highest answer was "missing sexual intimacy with a woman."[5] Both of these answers reveal that intimacy is the longing of the lesbian heart. Perhaps sexual intimacy was the only way the women could feel emotionally connected with another woman.

Alyssa's Story

Alyssa grew up in a strong churchgoing family in the Midwest. In fact, her parents had moved to the small town to help plant a church. In junior high Alyssa "felt different" and struggled with same-sex attractions all the way through college. She prayed to be delivered from her attractions but never shared them with anyone else. Toward the end of college, she met and married her husband, Eric. Secretly, she hoped that marriage and family would resolve her lifelong battle with attraction to women.

> I was sure of my complete healing, until shortly after we were married. I battled against thoughts and emotions and attractions. Still I held my silence and so did God. I was always alone; not one person ever knew me. Consequently I never felt really loved. I was who they—family and friends— wanted me to be. But they never knew the real me...what I felt like, what I battled, what I longed for. I was convinced that if they knew they wouldn't love me.

Alyssa found herself in a form of solitary confinement that was terribly painful. Instead of sharing her struggles earlier in life and gaining support from others, her choice to keep it to herself isolated her even further. Because she wasn't able to show herself ("the real me") to others who loved her, she wasn't able to receive their love. And now, she was both a wife and a mother of young children. Much more was at stake than when she was single.

Defensive Detachment

This form of emotional or relational solitary confinement has been called "defensive detachment." Bob Davies and Lori Rentzel, in their book *Coming Out of Homosexuality*, define defensive detachment as "When we self-protectively close ourselves off from intimate relationships."[6] Defensive detachment is common among same-sex attracted women. Nearly one-third of the women I surveyed "tend to avoid developing female friendships."[7]

To picture what defensive detachment is like, think of a dam. Our relational needs are the flowing water, and defensive detachment is the dam that holds back our needs. Because of our inability, fears, or previous rejection in relationships, we may stop up the flow of true intimacy in our lives. This wall is built to protect us from true vulnerability with others and creates great pressure—loneliness, sadness, and depression.

This is the state that Alyssa and so many of us have found ourselves in. Depending upon our resolve to never let anyone in, the dam may stay in place for quite some time. In fact, it may have been there so long—perhaps since childhood—that we may not be aware that we are defensively detached.

Bob Davies and Lori Rentzel further describe defensive detachment this way: "Most of us who struggle with defensive detachment are the last to believe we have a problem. In fact, we tend to be the ones who are proud of not having problems. If something does trouble us, we feel sure we can handle it by ourselves."[8]

The False Intimacy of Emotional Dependency

If defensive detachment is the wall of the dam, emotional dependency is one's tendency to open the floodgates when we finally find someone we can trust. The two are related, like opposite sides of a coin. *Eventually* someone who is detached will swing to attachment, but without the skills to attach in a healthy and adult way. Lori Rentzel, author of the short booklet, *Emotional Dependency,* defines emotional dependency as occuring "when the ongoing presence and nurturing of another is believed to be necessary for personal security."[9]

Mrs. Rentzel describes some symptoms of emotional dependency:

> [One] views other people as a threat to the relationship, prefers to spend time alone with this friend and becomes frustrated when this doesn't happen, becomes irrationally angry or depressed when the other withdraws slightly, loses interest in other friendships, experiences romantic or sexual feelings leading to fantasy about this person, is unwilling to make short- or long-term plans that do not include the other person...

And the list goes on.

Consider this illustration of the damlike properties of emotional dependency. The pressure of one's relational needs build up over time, and eventually a woman comes along who is sensitive and empathetic or has other characteristics we admire, and we decide to trust this one woman. Perhaps she is healthy in her personal life and walks up to the dam with a fire hose. Instead of discharging a small amount of relational needs, the defensively detached person will swing to emotional dependency, opening up a tidal wave of relational needs. So rather than the new friend finding a healthy, interdependent relationship, she finds an overwhelming wall of water about to engulf her.

At this point, if the friend is reasonably healthy, she may endure and place boundaries on the relationship (an ideal response), or she may back off completely. The trusted one may say to herself, *I'm going to be swallowed up by this vastness of need.* In an effort to preserve her own life, she will flee.

The common response of the wounded individual with a reservoir of relational needs is to say, "See! I knew I couldn't trust others." And thus, the self-protective cycle of defensive detachment begins again until the pressure builds too high. On the other hand, if that trusted one is herself needy in her own unique ways, she may feel flattered by the attention and exclusivity, and it may eventually lead to sexual sin.

Let's return to Alyssa's story to hear what this sounds like in a woman's life.

> It was in the midst of that pain and loneliness that Nicole entered my life. Our kids were the same age, she and her husband loved the Lord, and we had many common interests. She was safe, the safest person I had ever known. Compassion oozed out of her—she truly loved and accepted [others] where they were.
>
> It was six to nine months after we became friends that I told her about my struggles. I held my breath, but she never condemned me. Instead, she questioned me, loved me, and prayed for me. As you can imagine, Nicole became the most important person in my life. After all, she knew the "real" me and still loved me. It was the first genuine acceptance I had experienced in all my 39 years.

Her relationship was essentially set up for friendship idolatry or dependency from the beginning because Nicole was the only person who knew the real Alyssa. Not even Alyssa's husband had been given such an opportunity to know her as deeply. When I read Alyssa's letter further, I wasn't surprised to find that they had become sexually involved.

"Over the last couple of years," Alyssa wrote, "our friendship has been an unhealthy emotional mess...I depended upon her in every situation. I sought her opinion and told her my innermost thoughts. Because of this intimacy, we have periodically allowed this relationship to enter inappropriate physical dimensions."

Thankfully, today Alyssa is becoming free from her inner prison. Through her desperate search for help and change, she confided in her husband, parents, pastor, and another female Christian mentor. Her wall of silence has been broken, and she is receiving correction and love from a number of sources. Because of her failure, she is being set free—to live honestly and to walk out of her solitary confinement.

Healthy Female Friendships

"Okay," you say, "you've convinced me that avoiding relationships with women is a bad idea, and that depending on any one individual too heavily is not healthy. Now, how do I develop *healthy* friendships with other women?" In the rest of this chapter we'll learn how to build healthy friendships.

> When I talk to my closest female friends, I feel my soul being sunned and watered. (Dee Brestin).[10]

We'll discover some of the tools that will enable you to have reasonable expectations in your female friendships and help you avoid overwhelming others with tidal waves of relational needs.

In the summer of 2002, I taught a class about healthy female friendships with a dear friend, Lori Leander. I was especially excited because of her distinctly heterosexual perspective and also because she has learned much in her relationships with women—both the risks and rewards. She emphasized in the class, "Good friends truly are among life's greatest treasures, but you need to be discerning about whom you allow in your intimate circle." Lori continued, "Anytime you make yourself vulnerable to a meaningful friendship, you do make yourself vulnerable to potential pain. That is inherent in becoming vulnerable to someone else. However, it should be a calculated risk."

Different Levels of Friendship

Not every relationship will be or should be intimate. Jesus himself, God on Earth, had different levels of relationships with people. He related to the multitudes, His larger group of disciples, the handpicked 12 disciples, and His inner circle of the three closest disciples. I liken these different groups to acquaintances, friends, good friends, and intimate friends.

Acquaintances

In Jesus' life, *acquaintances* could be considered individuals who had heard him speak or who had shared a miraculous loaf of bread at the feeding of the 5000 (Matthew 14:14-21). This outermost sphere of relationships may include hundreds of people, from people you recognize at church to people you purchase groceries from at the store. This preliminary contact with others may or may not

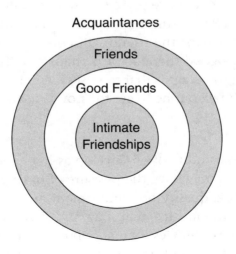

progress into friendship. You may be friendly with them, but you do not know them well, nor do they know you well.

Friends

The second grouping of relationships could be considered *friends*. We have made a deliberate attempt to get to know these people, and they have reciprocated to some degree. Initiating friendship among women is moving beyond simply greeting another woman to intentional contact: sharing coffee together, having dinner in a smaller group setting, or visiting after Bible study. The interpersonal commitment is greater but not significantly.

These women may be friends that you grew up with or coworkers that you share a coffee break with. This is the kind of relationship Jesus might have had with all of his followers. Some of his disciples were not steadfast and fled when He began talking about the more difficult truths (John 6:41-66).

You may easily have ten or more friends of this second level. This type of friendship is necessary as a stepping-stone for those who will later become more intimate friends. It's a good and relatively safe place to test and evaluate the qualities of your relationship before making any long-term commitments. Perhaps the friend will enter the next group at some point—good friends—or perhaps not. The wonderful thing about this stage is that the risks aren't too high because you've both taken time to get to know one another.

Good Friends

Good friends quite often develop as lives and/or interests intersect. You may have the pleasure of having five or more friends of this quality of commitment and trust. In developing good friendships, you may find that you both enjoy the same type of movies, similar hobbies, work interests, similar depth of commitment to God, or you may be going through similar stages in your life, for example: singleness, childrearing, or midlife.

When I asked the question, Have you been successful at establishing healthy long-term relationships with other women? three-fourths of the women I surveyed responded yes. When asked what setting helped to facilitate these relationships, two-thirds answered their "small group fellowship."[11] Almost one-half answered that Bible study groups had been a key to getting to know other women. In such settings, women's lives can intersect for more than a moment, and they can learn about each other's qualities and views in a safe group setting over a period of time before deciding to be vulnerable with one another.

Good friends are incredibly valuable: I may choose to selectively share with my good friends about my deepest fears, problems in marriage, or childrearing. Moving from acquaintance to friend and then to good friend takes time— perhaps a year or longer. True good friends develop neither overnight nor over a series of weeks. Commitment grows over a much longer period of time.

The 12 disciples may have been Jesus' good friends. Betrayal by a good friend, as Jesus was betrayed by Judas, is very painful. King David wrote about that same pain, "Even my close friend, whom I trusted, he who shared my bread, has lifted up his heel against me" (Psalm 41:9).

In times of hardship, personal tragedy, or success, we see the truest qualities of our friends. Drs. Les and Leslie Parrot quote Churton Collins in their book *Relationships 101:* "In prosperity our friends know us, in adversity we know our friends."[12] And Proverbs declares, "A friend loves at all times, and a brother is born for adversity" (Proverbs 17:17, NASB).

Intimate Friends

Intimate friends are a special category of their own. With approximately three intimate friends, our intimacy circle fills

> *Be courteous to all, but intimate with few, and let those few be well tried before you give them your confidence. True friendship is a plant of slow growth, and must undergo and withstand the shocks of adversity before it is entitled to the appellation (George Washington).*

up quickly. If you are a married woman, your husband should be within that circle. If we consider that we have more than three or four intimate friends that fit into our lives at any one time, we are probably mistaking the level of our friendships. Proverbs 18:24 states, "A man of many friends comes to ruin"(NASB). Again, true intimacy implies time to get to know each other, the safety to share confidences, and freedom to ask for counsel or perspective.

Evaluating how to proceed in developing friendships before diving in is essential! Unfortunately, in the case of same-sex attracted women, we may rush someone prematurely from acquaintance to intimate friend. In fact, attempting such a maneuver in the first meeting is not unheard of. If this occurs, watch out—emotional dependency may lead quickly to some unexpected results: jealousy, envy, anger, and depression.

True intimate friendships are timeless. I have several friendships with women across the country that I consider intimate friendships. Weeks or months may transpire between coversations, but we always seem to pick up where we left off and rarely have a difficult time slipping into a comfortable and often vulnerable conversation. Julie is a perfect example of such a friend. When I phone her or she phones me, time seems to have stood still between conversations. We can support and care for each other though we are five states apart. That doesn't mean we should neglect our closest friends, for as the Parrots write, "Even strong friendships require watering, or they are sure to shrivel up and blow away."[13]

In Jesus' life and ministry on Earth, perhaps the three disciples—Peter, James, and John—fit into that circle of intimate friends. These were the three that Jesus specifically selected to go with Him on the Mount of Transfiguration in Mark 9:2-4. There the three saw Jesus in His glory—He was not hidden, but rather His authority was revealed.

What about Best Friends?

As my friend Lori explained at the Exodus 2002 conference,

> Even from a heterosexual viewpoint, it is not really a good idea to have someone that you crown your best friend. Each friend is gifted in and enriches our lives in different ways. Second, if you have three to five close friends and one gets crowned my best friend, what happens to the other close friends? Probably they will start backing off and not investing in your relationship. And finally, because other women are backing off, that leaves you and your "best friend" isolated in your relationship.

From an ex-gay perspective, constantly looking for a best friend as the solution to relational needs points us directly back to emotional dependency (which could also be called friendship idolatry). Remember the example of the dam versus the normal relational pressure of a fire hose. Women overcoming same-sex attraction can believe that intimacy with one woman is what they need. But we must not worship another imperfect creation as the answer to all our needs.

Do you secretly say to yourself, *If I could just find that best friend I would be satisfied*? If so, instead of seeking out the perfect woman, seek out the only perfect person—God Himself. Proverbs 18:24 explains, "There is a friend who sticks closer than a brother." Well, guess who that friend is? Who stands head and shoulders above all the competition?

> For who in the skies above can compare with the LORD? Who is like the LORD among the heavenly beings? In the council of the holy ones God is greatly feared; he is more awesome than all who surround him. O LORD God Almighty, who is like you? You are mighty, O LORD, and your faithfulness surrounds you (Psalm 89:6-8).

Did you know that the Lord will take you into His confidence? Proverbs 3:32 says, "the LORD detests a perverse man but takes the upright into his confidence." Why should you trade such intimacy with the most reliable, purposeful, pure, and incredibly beautiful Being that exists for the illusion that emotional dependency offers? This would be like trading diamonds for mere gravel. As Jeremiah declares,

> Cursed is the one who trusts in man, who depends on flesh for his strength and whose heart turns away from the LORD.... But blessed is the man who trusts in the LORD, whose confidence is in him. He will be like a tree planted by the water that sends out its roots by the stream.... It has no worries in a year of drought and never fails to bear fruit (Jeremiah 17:5,7-8).

The only reward of virtue is virtue; the only way to have a friend is to be one (Ralph Waldo Emerson).

Learning to be a Friend

Truly, the only way to have friends is to be one to others. But friendship skills are not inborn, and our families may not have modeled them for us, so we need to consciously develop them. We will have to learn from our successes and failures as we practice these critical skills. Remember that as we practice, the potential rewards are incredible. We must learn the art of engaging others in conversation, listening, asking good questions, serving others, and keeping commitments.

Engaging others in conversation is an art form indeed. Some of us avoid small talk when getting to know others, but that can greatly limit our interactions with them. For instance, when my boys are starting a new school year, I enjoy getting to know the parents of other children in their classes. If I refused to talk with others about basic aspects of their lives, I might never get to know them at all. Standing in line with other parents for registration, we asked each other questions such as, What class is your daughter or son in? Do you have any other children? These simple questions can lead to more meaningful conversations.

After several pleasant interactions, we often progress to topics of general concern to wives and mothers, even asking parenting advice from each other. And eventually, after getting to know each other through basic conversations, we begin to talk about our feelings.

In order to even begin engaging others in conversation, we must participate in activities that place us in group settings with others. As Brenda Hunter points out, "We need to pursue our own interests. We will be happier and more fulfilled if we are chasing our dreams and snaring them rather than waiting for someone to come along and validate our worthiness."[14]

When getting to know other women, we should not reach for intimacy too quickly. Sharing our deepest needs or most troubling experiences is not wise in early relationships. I call it "dumping" because this practice makes others feel as if you just piled sandbags on their shoulders. Dr. Hunter wrote, "Only needy people spill secrets indiscriminately."[15]

Listening to others is a critical friendship skill. And this skill goes hand in hand with asking good questions. As my friend Lori says, "Interesting people are people who are interested." In other words, other people will be interested in getting to know a woman who is interested in them. If we do not listen to and ask questions of our women friends but rather share a nonstop monologue about our lives, we are being self-centered. Potential friends may come to believe that we are not really interested in them after all.

Asking questions is an art. Some questions can be answered with a simple yes or no; others probe about how the other person thinks or feels about something. You can respond to your friend's statement about something or someone by asking, "Oh really...why do you feel that way?" Then stop and listen. Don't prepare your next statement or question ahead of time. As Proverbs 18:13 says, "He who answers before listening—that is his folly and shame."

Serving others is another way to move beyond our own world and troubles and to express concern for others. Send an encouraging note when a friend is going through a difficult time. Prepare food for one who is sick. Such actions can be powerful demonstrations of concern and friendship. Acknowledging someone else's kindness is also important. Thank-you notes have existed for generations for a reason—they acknowledge another's graciousness.

When a friend invites you to her home for dinner, ask her, "What can I bring?" or "How can I help?" If she answers "Nothing," bring a hospitality gift that she may enjoy—a jar of preserves, gourmet accent oil, or something symbolic of the season of the year, such as an inexpensive Christmas ornament or a pumpkin candle.

Some women serve with wrong motives but may not be aware of their feelings. Avoid giving what your friends may consider romantic or expensive gifts. Choose something other than roses or cards declaring your affection. A good question to ask yourself is, "How would I feel if a man gave me (or my friend) these gifts?" Another motive-revealing question is, Do I always (or often) give gifts to the same friend?

Friends also follow through on their commitments. If you say you will go to a movie with someone, keep your word. If you make commitments rashly, learn to build some time into the process. Tell your friend you will let her know later, and give an approximate time when you will let her know. Don't forget to call her back by the agreed upon date or time to inform her of your decision. If you decline the invitation, you do not need to explain why, but the more intimate the friendship, the more likely you will be to explain.

What Qualities to Look for in Friendships

So what are good characteristics to look for in a friend? In my opinion, this is number one: You must be headed in the same spiritual direction. If you want to grow, you need friendships with other women who are spiritually supportive and will help you mature. Honesty, trustworthiness, and commitment to the Lord are also solid attributes to seek out in other women. Find friends who refuse to gossip. As Dee Brestin wrote in her book, *The Friendships of Women,* "We will become like our closest friends."[16]

He who walks with the wise grows wise, but a companion of fools suffers harm (Proverbs 13:20).

I value a couple of other character qualities in my friends. They speak the truth, even when I do not want to hear it. They empathize with me in my pain, frustration, or sorrow. In other words, I value friends who are real, and I hope to offer these qualities to my friends in return. "Faithful are the wounds of a friend, but deceitful are the kisses of an enemy" (Proverbs 27:6 NASB). Cicero wrote in 50 B.C., "It appears that genuine friendship cannot possibly exist where one of the parties is unwilling to hear the truth and the other equally indisposed to speak it."

Reciprocity or give-and-take in friendship is important. This applies to conversations (the friendship should not focus on the events or concerns of just one person) as well as the time and effort involved in pursuing or maintaining the relationship. If one person is always calling and the other friend never initiates, then the friendship is unbalanced. If one person is willing to drive across town to visit but the other is not willing to drive down the street, then the energy and effort are not balanced.

When a friendship is not reciprocal, someone will not feel valued. One solution is to slow down and exert less energy. Another is to ask the individual about the discrepancy. Perhaps she is encountering issues with depression, loss of job, or other things that are making friendship difficult for her. Or maybe she simply isn't interested. Depending on the circumstances, you may choose to be patient, or you may simply want to reconsider how close you wish to get.

> *In each of my friends there is something that only some other friend can fully bring out. By myself I am not large enough to call the whole person into activity; I want other lights than my own to show all his facets. Hence true friendship is the least jealous of loves (C. S. Lewis).*

Warning Signs on the Road to Intimacy

Here are a few "red flags" that should slow down a developing friendship. Anyone who doesn't heed these warning signs can be deeply hurt. First, watch out for those who gossip. Dee Brestin records this comment from Gail MacDonald: "I usually find if a person easily talks about other people in a negative way, I can assume she's going to do the same thing about me."[17]

Other signs to watch for are envy and jealousy. Instead of being able to rejoice with our successes, some people may become competitive with us. Instead of appreciating us as individuals and encouraging us in our own personal growth, someone who is competitive, envious, or jealous of us may seek to stunt our personal growth. Jealousy constricts relationships and does not enrich them. As my friend Lori shared, "If you love someone and have their best interests at heart, then you share in their victories and accomplishments instead of feeling threatened by them."

A friend who is jealous may seek to isolate us from other friendships. A real friend doesn't harbor resentment when we develop other close relationships. In her book *In the Company of Women,* Brenda Hunter identifies this tendency as a toxin.

> The second key toxin in any friendship is choking, clinging dependency. Friends control others by "bleeding the life out of them." We can't look to friends to fill us up—to provide something we don't possess....Only when we learn to love ourselves and have compassion for ourselves will we be able to have healthy friendships.[18]

By way of contrast, Lori Rentzel writes that in healthy friendships, both friends "...are happy when one friend hits it off with another person. In a good friendship, we desire to see the other reach his or her full potential, developing new interests and skills."[19]

Accepting Our Friend's Limitations and Faults

"When you have a variety of friendships," Lori Leander shared, "you tend to put less pressure on one to meet all your needs. Therefore you can be more accepting of their weaknesses and shortcomings. You definitely need to cut them some slack for being human."

For example, if you have a friend who has difficulty being on time, don't rely on them to be punctual for an important event. If you have heard your friend utter secrets about others behind their backs, don't be shocked if she does it to you. This is an example of a warning sign on the road to intimacy, which we have already discussed. Nonetheless, you must recognize that your friends are imperfect people—just as you are—and that some days their weaknesses may show more glaringly than others. Bearing with another's weaknesses is easier if we have chosen our friends wisely in the first place.

Boundaries That Keep a Friendship Healthy

As we've already seen, we should learn to develop friendships slowly. This is particularly wise for the ex-gay woman. A woman overcoming same-sex attraction and developing healthy friendships with other women may experience confusion between excitement about the relationship and sexual attraction. In such a case, the woman needs to slow down the friendship enough to not encourage those old feelings. She will need time to sort through them.

When we make new friends, we should also take the time to maintain dear and established friendships. Invest in your current relationships. Keep up with other friends separately and maintain your individuality. A broad base of friendships will help you through times of temptation and attraction.

Also remember not to confide in your friend that you are struggling with attraction toward her. You may wish to review this topic in chapter 7, Overcoming Temptation. The reasons are tried and true.

Jenna's Experience

Jenna is a woman that I met through my survey research. She is from the East Coast and is in her mid-30s. Although she has struggled for most of her life with same-sex attraction, Jenna has not acted on those feelings. After consulting with me, she began seeing a female Christian therapist to honestly work through her feelings. In a way, she is at the beginning of her journey in dealing with her long-held sexual attractions toward women. Jenna described her confused feelings to me:

> It seems my lesbian feelings are more of an issue of intimacy than sexuality. But I am so confused by it, Anne. I have developed a very strong bond with Olivia [her counselor], as I think you were saying would be a good thing in order to work through these feelings. But my feelings can be scary sometimes because they are so strong. But I know that they are so unreal, in the sense that they are not and cannot be reality. Olivia will never be my mother. And it's not just her...there has been a pattern of women who I am attracted to, personality-wise, people I admire along the way. Right now it is Olivia and another woman friend at church. With Olivia, just talking about my feelings or our relationship...well, I can hardly think sometimes. I slip back to the age of three and just sit mesmerized by the thought of being close to her.
>
> What confuses me is that sometimes I feel those feelings physiologically, and they seem like "sexual" feelings. And so I feel stuck, feeling safe in her presence as a three-year-old, but then also having these other feelings that come along with it. I am not intending to feel sexual feelings and I am not thinking sexually, but there they are.

I encouraged Jenna that this is a normal process in dealing with same-sex attraction and that she should sort through her feelings. Her craving for intimacy and connection with a safe female caretaker at a very young age had not been met. Those desires were still with her in her mid-30s, jumbled with adult feelings of admiration, excitement, and adrenaline, which were triggering a sexual response. In a sense, Jenna was both a three-year-old and an intelligent, articulate, grown woman.

But as she persevered through the challenge of relating to her counselor and the woman at church, she began to unravel feelings that had been tightly connected for all of her adult years. She began to feel, to grieve what was lost at such a young age, and to deal with her little girl longings. She also began to understand her need for emotional intimacy with other women as part of her God-designed nature.

Christine Sneeringer, a former lesbian and director of an Exodus ministry in Florida, put it this way, "If you notice something about another female—like she's pretty or her personality is so attractive—the thought that may immediately follow is *Arggh, I am such a lesbian.*" In other words, Christine is mentioning the confusion of admiration and sexual attraction.

Christine remembers her first close female friendship after leaving the lesbian lifestyle.

> My very first, close, straight-woman friend was the hardest one. That was the most challenging because it was scary realizing that as we got closer, I had nothing to compare this intimacy with except my old lesbian relationships. One time, this friend and I went out to eat after church and I looked in her eyes and thought to myself, *She has beautiful eyes.* I remember feeling bad that I thought she had beautiful eyes. It took me some time to realize that straight women will compliment and admire other straight women. Now I realize that other women admire and compliment each other all the time—"You look great," or "You look radiant today." In the past, I would have felt like a lesbian even noticing another woman's beauty.

With these ideas in mind, give yourself time to sort through the jumbled feelings of admiration and attraction. Admiration is commonly mistaken for attraction simply because we have always made that jump before. Now, more than 15 years after beginning to work through those jumbled feelings of lesbian attraction, I notice women admiring each other all the time, building each other up in casual conversation. I often compliment other women on their clothing, their eye color, or some other appealing feature.

Our friends are among our life's greatest treasures. They help us negotiate the difficult hurdles of life....In their presence, we laugh about what drove us crazy hours before; with them we cry without shame, knowing we will be understood (Brenda Hunter, Ph.D).[20]

One evening I attended a Christmas symphony with my husband and was dressed in an elegant green dress with a purple silk bolero jacket over my shoulders. I felt gorgeous, and apparently I looked it. Men and women alike were giving me admiring glances. But the women more often walked up to me and said something such as, "Wow, you look incredibly beautiful," or "What a gorgeous dress!" Straight women compliment straight women freely.

If you prioritize loving God, keep your relationship with Him first, and then concern yourself with others, you will succeed in dealing with emotional dependency. Just remember to give yourself time to learn and practice friendship skills. We need grace while we learn and grow because we will make mistakes. If you use mistakes to gain understanding instead of browbeating yourself, you will learn these key friendship skills and become an appealing friend.

Don't fear female friendships. They are God's rich blessings for you. Coming out of lesbianism doesn't mean you will give up intimacy. You will actually discover the *right* way to enjoy close female relationships with security and confidence.

9

Men: Friendships, Singleness, and Marriage

A Safe Distance

Once we same-sex attracted women have learned how to have intimate, long-term relationships with other women and fit in the female community, we may begin to look at men in a new and different way. Although our methods may have differed, many of us have probably kept males at a safe distance for much of our lives. This will remain an appropriate attitude as a woman leaving lesbianism learns to embrace her feminine identity and begins the process toward wholeness as a woman. We cannot appropriately relate to the opposite sex until we properly relate to those who are the same as ourselves. For this reason, I do not advise dating men before knowing who we are as women.

See, a king will reign in righteousness and rulers will rule with justice. Each man will be like a shelter from the wind and a refuge from the storm, like streams of water in the desert and the shadow of a great rock in a thirsty land (Isaiah 32:1-2).

Women who have experienced abuse at the hands of men may have concluded that all men are abusive, sexual predators, or vile. Once we begin to deal with abuse issues (discussed in chapter 6), we may also realize that some men *can* be trusted.

If our past pain hasn't been resolved, we may choose to maintain a safe distance from men. Some women do this by overeating, and others try looking as masculine as the guys in order to stave off attractions. Thirty percent of the women in my survey said that they deal with pain by overeating. One woman, who I believe represents many, said she discovered her motivation for being overweight when she began gaining weight again after successfully losing several pounds. She told me the prospect of men finding her attractive caused her to quit dieting and put back on all the weight she had fought so hard to lose.

Penny Dalton, co-director of Whosoever Will Ministry, Exodus board member, and former lesbian, said she used "caustic remarks that would cut men to the heart" if they made an advance toward her.

> If it hadn't been for Christ coming into my life, I never would have worked through the forgiveness process with my father because of incest. I never would have come to the conclusion that men aren't all the same. God has brought me, over a number of years, to a place of understanding that there is another half of humanity. That His creation, male and female, is delightful and complements one another.

This isn't meant to be a blanket indictment that all women dealing with same-sex attraction do not relate well with men. But if you look closely you may notice that many of us are relating at a safe emotional distance. Safe relationships with men are platonic. They are friendships with spouses of friends, ex-gay men, and others who are unavailable or uninterested in pursuing a more intimate relationship. Being buddies or pals with men can reflect that a woman personally identifies herself as just another guy.

I know that I experienced that sense of platonic safety with men in college and beyond. Because I struggled with same-sex attraction, I felt very comfortable relating to men on their level, talking with them, sharing interests, doing fun activities together, and even hugging them. However, I never expected the response I so often received from these single college guys. During those years, a handful of young men that I felt such commonality with had physical attractions toward me and asked me out on dates. I was always surprised and wondered, *How did* that *happen?*

Christine Sneeringer had similar experiences in her college years.

> A guy tennis pro was my best friend when I was first on my journey out of homosexuality. We'd do all kinds of stuff together when I was in college. But at one point he sat me down and said, "I need to ask you a question—I just need to know if you would be interested in dating me." And I looked at him as if to say, *Are you crazy?* That had *never* occurred to me. I felt like saying, "No—that's gross. That would be like kissing my brother." It was so funny. I just couldn't understand why he said that.

Some Men Can Be Trusted

The thought that some men could be trusted had never occurred to me. One very hot, humid summer in San Antonio, Texas, I attended my first Exodus conference. I was walking alone at about 11 P.M. to meet with some female friends after an evening session when my worst fear confronted me. The path I had chosen was empty until a man began walking the same route behind me. I felt like running because his walking pace was faster than mine and he was gaining on me. Instead, I stopped and turned around to face him and let him pass.

Fortunately for me, he was a male ministry director for Exodus who greeted me warmly. He then recounted seeing me earlier in the worship time, surrounded by the men of my ministry, and declared, "It was so beautiful to see you surrounded by those men. It looked like they were surrounding you with protection." I was baffled by several things: First, that this stranger was a friendly face, then that I should need the protection of men, and finally by such a foreign thought that men could possibly be protectors. I hardly remember thanking him, because I was so stunned. But I do remember thinking, *Maybe some men can be trusted.*

Men and Women Are Not That Different... Or Are They?

When we accept our sameness with other women and appreciate who we are as women, we begin to understand the differences between men and women.

> *When men and women agree, it is only in their conclusions; their reasons are always different (George Santayana).[1]*

After I graduated from an Exodus live-in discipleship program in 1990, I remained in the area and continued to attend the church in which I had become comfortable. I also became more involved in the women's monthly socials and annual retreats, helping out where I could. One day, I realized that these women accepted me and treated me like a sister. I also realized that I had come to *like* being a woman.

I understood in my heart that God had deliberately made me a woman and will always treasure me as one. Somehow along the way I had subtly changed my point of view and had embraced my own gender with a deep sense of contentment and satisfaction.

At this same time I became less comfortable being "pals" with men. I came to realize that wrestling, hugging, and even patting the shoulder of ex-gay men was beginning to be unfamiliar territory. I was beginning to relate to men with my newfound femininity, recognizing that we were different. Something was changing.

In the past, I didn't hesitate to "pal around" with a man as if I was another guy, but now I was beginning to see our differences. I felt as if I was looking out a window at a scene I had viewed all my life but never really seen before. I experienced an awakening.

Men are *weird and different from me,* I concluded. They also became intriguing. With women, on the other hand, I now felt camaraderie, a profound sameness.

I began to have "crushes" on some attentive ex-gay men. My feelings were almost silly—I felt like a seventh-grade girl. Puberty seemed to hit me at the age of 25!

Men—*Practically* a Different Species

Since marrying my love, my husband John, in 1992, we have worked hard to communicate with and understand each other. During the first year of our marriage we went to a Christian therapist with problems that we thought were related to our homosexual pasts. We had to learn how to work through our disagreements. I also wanted to run from conflict until I cooled down, whereas John wanted to resolve our disagreement immediately regardless of how steamed we were.

I will never forget our counselor laughing aloud at us and then telling us with amusement, "John...Anne...these disagreements you're having are all related to the differences between men and women. Every marriage goes through these challenges as the husband and wife learn to understand each other."

Since then we have been in several different couples' Bible studies, and as we get to know the other couples who don't share our homosexual background, we see that they are working through similar issues. Men and women are distinct. Raising three boys has confirmed this conclusion in many ways.

This reality is reflected in the popular book by John Gray, *Men Are from Mars, Women Are from Venus*. People so identified with his concepts of gender differences that he has been successful in creating a number of other products, including a video, a TV series, and even a board game by Mattel.

Of course our bodies are different, but the way we process information is dramatically different as well and has been since we were in the womb. Males underwent a testosterone hormone wash six or seven weeks after conception. As Dr. James Dobson writes in his book, *Bringing up Boys,*

> In a real sense, this "hormonal bath," as it is sometimes called, actually damages the walnut-shaped brain and alters its structure in many ways. Even its color changes. The corpus callosum, which is the rope of nerve fibers that connects the two hemispheres, is made less efficient. That limits the number of electrical transmissions that can flow from one side of the brain to the other, which will have lifelong implications.[2]

One of the repercussions of that early hormonal bath is that men tend to focus on one thing at a time, while women can more easily multitask. As therapist Michael Gurian writes, in his nationally acclaimed book *The Wonder of Boys,*

> This difference [the lower connectivity of the corpus callosum] is a primary reason males are so "task-oriented," testing out as less able than females to do a number of different kinds of tasks

at once; and why males react to interruptions in their thinking with more of a sense of invasion than females tend to, and combined with testosterone-based aggression, more forcefully."[3]

I have seen this daily while raising my boys. They must accomplish at least three tasks before we can leave for school: brush their teeth, make their bed, put their shoes on, and... oh, don't forget the backpack. Instead of remembering and following my little list, our six-year-old may get one or two of the items done and then become distracted. He really is trying, but he gets sidetracked. Instead of getting frustrated or angry, I try to remember his brain is constructed that way. So I now check on him after one or two of the tasks are complete and remind him of the rest.

Dr. Dobson sums up the impact of testosterone in this way:

> Most experts believe boys' tendency to take risks, to be more assertive, to fight and compete, to argue, to boast, and to excel at certain skills, such as problem solving, math, and science, is directly linked to the way the brain is hardwired and to the presence of testosterone. This may explain why boys have "ants in their pants" when they are in the classroom and why teachers call them little "wiggly worms."...It's just the way God made them.[4]

My husband and I decided not to give Timmy, our first son, any guns to play with—even squirt guns. We had the misconception that gun play would lead to aggression later on. Our little boy naturally turned my kitchen spatula into a weapon. You would have been amazed at the sound effects emanating from that spatula. We didn't take long to realize that this was just the way little boys are. Later on in life, if he is well cared for and directed, his natural desire to fight the "bad guys" will lead to his ability to protect those he holds dear.

Other hormonal and brain differences also make men different from women. As Dr. Gurian notes in his book, one difference is "a neurotransmitter, serotonin, which inhibits aggressive behavior, and which exists in higher levels in girls than boys."[5]

Dr. Dobson adds, "If testosterone is the gasoline that powers the brain, serotonin slows the speed and helps one steer."[6]

Lest we think poorly of God's design of maleness, I will add this comment from Dr. Dobson about the complementary nature of the two sexes:

> Consider again the basic tendencies of maleness and femaleness. Because it is the privilege and blessing of women to bear children, they are inclined toward predictability, stability, security, caution, and steadiness....The female temperament lends itself to nurturance, caring, sensitivity, tenderness, and compassion.
>
> Men, on the other hand, have been designed for a different role. They value change, opportunity, risk, speculation, and adventure. They are designed to provide for their families physically and to protect them from harm and danger.[7]

Singleness or Marriage?

Even though you may be dealing with same-sex attraction, you may be wondering, *Do I have to get married?* My answer is unambiguous—absolutely not. In fact, if you do not want to get married, you most certainly should not marry. Avoiding a marital commitment is better than trying to get out of one later. Doing so would break not only a covenant before God but also a man's heart.

Or you may wonder, *Would getting married prove that I have overcome same-sex attraction?* Again I answer, no. Marriage is not proof of change. And if you choose to marry, you should do so for the right reasons. Perhaps he is your "soul-mate," maybe you couldn't imagine your future without him, or he could be your best friend, who holds your heart. We will look closer at marriage after working through same-sex issues later in the chapter.

If you're wondering, *Which is better, singleness or marriage?* consider what the apostle Paul had to say about this very issue:

> Because of the present crisis, I think that it is good for you to remain as you are. Are you married? Do not seek a divorce. Are you unmarried? Do not look for a wife....
>
> An unmarried woman or virgin is concerned about the Lord's affairs: Her aim is to be devoted to the Lord in both body and spirit. But a married woman is concerned about the affairs of this world—how she can please her husband. I am saying this for your own good, not to restrict you, but that you may live in a right way in undivided devotion to the Lord (1 Corinthians 7:26-27, 34-35).

On the other hand, God not only designed marriage but also ordained the marital relationship between man and woman (Genesis 2:24-25, Matthew 19:5-6).

Penny Dalton, who is single and in her 50s, shared this about the single life:

> The purpose of my singleness is to be single-minded for Christ. The excitement I have in knowing what Christ has done in my life is that I am comfortable in me. I've been redeemed for relationship with God first and others second. I now

feel equally comfortable with men and with women. I know that I relate properly with women, having healthy relationships with women. I know that I am a whole woman in Christ and that I can relate in healthy, holy ways to both men and women.

What About Friendships with Men?

I am certain that ex-gay women can have platonic friendships with men, but once we are moving on in our wholeness as women, we must be more careful how we relate to men. Whether they are married or single, we need to keep greater boundaries with men than ever before. We have to be careful not to be too physical with them. For example, we learn to use the A-frame hug (where just your shoulders and neck touch) or the side hug when greeting them. If your male friend is married, your friendship should be primarily with his spouse and secondarily with the man. That way, you are not challenging his marriage: rather, you are respecting it.

Healthy, rewarding relationships are built on the following: a strong sense of personal identity, a thriving self-esteem, a personal sense of purpose, the ability to commit to things outside oneself, mutual respect, and good, old-fashioned courage (Drs. Les and Leslie Parrott).[8]

If he is single, take care not to invest too much time with him. If he is heterosexual, he could easily begin to have feelings for you that you may not reciprocate. Spend time with him in group settings, particularly if you are not interested in your friendship moving onto the next possible stage.

As a married woman, I enjoy friendships with my girlfriends' spouses. When we go out to dinner as couples, I thoroughly enjoy the conversations we have. I love venturing off into theological discussions or dissecting a social theory. You may have guessed that I love to banter a bit and rattle off ideas. So I find satisfying fellowship with men but only in certain contexts. As a married woman, I would not go out to dinner alone with another man. That would be inappropriate, and we are instructed by Scripture to avoid the appearance of evil (1 Thessalonians 5:22 KJV).

Am I Ready to Date?

John and I have taught several classes on the topic of knowing whether one is ready to date the opposite sex. This question is often asked by ex-gay men because their very nature as men is to act. But I think this information is helpful to women as well. Many women seeking to overcome same-sex attraction have asked me via e-mail or letters about dating men. Usually they inquire when a man is interested in dating them.

Immature love says, "I love you because I need you." Mature love says, "I need you because I love you" (Erich Fromm).[9]

Here are a few things to consider from an ex-gay perspective. If you have been dealing deliberately and seriously with your same-sex issues for less than one year, I suggest that you should not date yet. In fact, when I was in an intensive, yearlong Exodus discipleship program, the rule was no dating during that year. This guideline helped us to keep our focus on some very difficult issues in our lives.

Have women generally become somewhat boring to you now because you sense your commonality with them? If so, you may be ready to work through any unresolved feelings toward important men in your life such as your dad. If instead, you are often attracted to other women sexually, consumed with your female emotional relationships, or filled with disdain for straight women, this is not a good time to begin dating a man. Being engrossed in female relationships is natural when overcoming same-sex attraction, but romance with a man shouldn't enter the picture until you have been in the "sorority" of women for a while—long enough for you to feel comfortable in your female identity.

Are you unsure of your feelings toward a particular man? If you are uncertain of your interest or are uninterested, then don't continue to spend time alone with him. Be honest with him about where you are and let him off the hook. Toying with men's hearts isn't fair.

Are you interested in getting married? If not, why bother to date? I remember when John was first expressing an interest in me. I knew I didn't want to date just anyone. And after spending time with different men in group settings, I knew I was interested in John. I also knew I wouldn't date for sport and that this was potentially very serious. It shook me at that time to think that our relationship could very well lead to marriage. Somehow I hadn't even really imagined that outcome. But I was interested—very interested. What an exciting time!

I must add that I was very satisfied with my single life at that time. When John came calling, I approached our relationship as a secure person, not looking for validation through dating.

Dating, Engagement, and Marriage

If your friendship with a man may lead to dating and beyond, you are probably contemplating disclosing your personal history to him. I highly recommend that before engagement you share with him about your past and any lingering issues. Most men may feel a sense of intimacy with you and relief for the opportunity to admit their own past sexual failings.

With John, I had the privilege of dating a man who already knew

The right person can not and will not make your life complete. Once you have accepted that fact, you will be eligible for a happy, fulfilling relationship (Drs. Les and Leslie Parrott).[10]

about my past, and I knew about his. Even so, we had to be honest with each other about how our pasts may still be affecting us. We asked each other hard questions such as, *To what extent do you still deal with same-sex attractions?* We also shared with each other about past same-sex sexual relationships—not graphic details, but a summary of our past and present relationships with those individuals.

If you have resolved much of your same-sex attraction but still experience occasional temptation, you are not necessarily disqualified from dating and marriage. But how often do you feel the tug of same-sex sexual attraction? How do you deal with it? Since men commonly deal with sexual temptation, ask him tough questions too. If you move toward engagement, these questions will become vital. Both of you need to know beforehand with whom you are becoming more intimate.

Sexuality isn't the only part of your life to talk about with a man you begin dating. You will need to consider how each of you thinks about managing finances, attending church, having children, and relating to family and in-laws.

Are you in agreement concerning eternity and theology? The Bible warns about Christians dating non-Christians (2 Corinthians 6:14, 1 Corinthians 7:39). I have known heterosexual women who have "missionary dated," and now they are enduring the heartache of not knowing if their beloved husbands will be with them in eternity. This is too painful a route to go. You will be wise to avoid it.

> *If you fail to address your hurts from previous relationships and seek healing, you are destined to replay the pain again and again in future relationships (Drs. Les and Leslie Parrott).*[11]

Deal with any past sexual abuse before getting married. That doesn't mean your marriage will not be affected, but you give your potential marriage the best chance to survive by addressing areas in which you have been wounded. If you don't deal with sexual abuse from your past, it will interfere with your ability to bond sexually with your husband. Therapist Jan Frank and her husband, Don, wrote a book on this topic entitled, *Unclaimed Baggage: Dealing with the Past on Your Way to a Stronger Marriage*.[12] I strongly recommend it for women who have been abused and are considering marriage.

The foundation for a good marriage has many aspects—more than can be covered in one chapter in this book. For that reason, if marriage is an option for you, I strongly recommend you read some of the many excellent books available. Authors I highly recommend include the Drs. Parrott, Stephen Arterburn, Dr. Dobson, Dan Allender, Al Janssen, Gary Smalley, John Trent, and Larry Crabb, to name just a few. I also recommend you and your prospective mate meet with your pastor and attend a premarital class. Just remember to look beyond your passion for a moment and build a good foundation for the future.

I remember the day John and I went on a first "real date" to the Napa Wine Country in California. I know he was just as nervous as I was—neither one of us could eat our lunch before we set out on our long drive. After a while, we were able to move past our nervousness, and he reached out to hold my hand while he drove. Talk about a spark! I never knew holding another person's hand could move me so. We actually had to set up touch guidelines after that date. What an exciting time that was!

> *Once a spark of attraction catches flame, it can quickly become a raging fire of unreasonable passion. It's best not to make decisions while engulfed in its heat! (Drs. Les and Leslie Parrott).*[13]

The Bible commands us to avoid premarital sex. However, if you have been sexually active in the past, make sure you have remained sexually pure for at least two years before getting married. Hopefully, you have not had sexual relationships outside of marriage. But if this is not the case, Christ can restore a sense of virginity.

When John and I married, I was nervous about the wedding night. But my reservations were resolved ever so quickly. When John and I were sexually intimate after marriage, I remember waking up the next morning expecting to feel the shame or regret of sin (probably because that had happened in my other relationships). But it was absent. As Genesis 2:25 says, "The man and his wife were both naked, and they felt no shame." The experience crowned our marriage union with God's blessing. After all, we were participating in His design.

Also, I had been given the destructive advice from a married straight woman that if my husband was interested in sex and I was not, I should just go ahead and "do it" out of love for him. That may have worked for her, but as a former victim of sexual abuse, that scared me to no end. I was willing to participate, but I felt so honored and cherished by my husband when he responded, "Anne, if you are not in the mood, then neither am I. I can wait." John didn't use a power trip to push me into sexual intimacy. That was very healing for me. It reinforced my value as a woman and showed how much John loved me.

What If I'm Married and Dealing with Same-Sex Attraction?

Without a doubt, dealing with same-sex attraction while married is even more challenging. If you have never discussed your feelings for women with your husband, he may feel betrayed and angry with you when you do disclose your struggle. If you have children, particularly young children, this revelation may rock their world. Difficulty between Mommy and Daddy tends to create insecurity for them. Their world depends upon the stability of the relationship between their parents.

No doubt you will want to consider carefully when and how to share your struggles with your husband. You should also reaffirm your commitment. Are you willing to work through these feelings and not abandon your husband (and family)? Be prepared to answer this important question honestly—to yourself and also to him. We advised one married woman to wait to disclose her struggles until she had made up her mind whether or not to fight for her marriage.

I know of several young married mothers who have battled same-sex attraction in order to restore their marriages. Eventually, the truth of a wife's attractions comes out. When that happens, be prepared to empathize with your spouse, explain that the roots of same-sex attraction are actually nonsexual, and humbly listen to his frustration and pain. Keep in mind that the most common reaction from men is anger. And they often express anger for any number of feelings—betrayal, hurt, and pain. They cry less commonly but if anything could bring a man to tears, this might be it. The hardest part for him may be that you didn't confide in him before.

I must say, by way of encouragement, that in my years of lay counseling, I have found rejection from a spouse very uncommon in these cases. Of course, the possibility always exists, but rejection has been rare in my experience ministering to married women. Yes, husbands experience a painful period of grief, but many are willing to walk through the healing process with their wife. I also know of quite a few restored marriages that have grown stronger through this painful but important process.

One word to the wise in this situation: Don't expect your husband to understand your feelings. Rather, be ready to offer reading material which provides information for him. You can order cassette tapes from the Exodus office on all sorts of topics, including "I Have Something to Tell You: Successful Disclosure," and "Lesbianism and the Married Woman." The testimonies of men and women are available on audiotape as well.[14]

Jane Boyer's Experience

In chapter 7, I shared with you a portion of Jane Boyer's story. She received the Lord Jesus Christ at the young age of five in a home with an abusive, alcoholic father and a weak mother. Despite the pain that several different men represented in her life, she married at a young age without resolving her past experiences. Her internal conflicts eventually drove her to live a double life as a married Christian woman and a lesbian. She somehow managed to keep her worlds from colliding for approximately five years, but one day the truth came to light.

Mike, her husband, returned home from an extended trip to find a love letter on his kitchen table addressed to Jane from her female lover. His immediate response was to cry out in prayer, "God, You've got to help me. Look what's happened to my marriage! I need You to step in and do something about this!" Jane recounted,

> Within the hour Mike called me at the office. "Jane, you need to make up your mind. You can't go on living like this. But let me warn you. If you decide to live the gay life, I will not allow our children to be raised in that kind of environment."
>
> I knew he was right. I was faced with making the most difficult decision of my life: choosing between the man I married—for whom I had no desire—and the woman whom I felt I could not live without. I had to choose between the gay community where I felt support and acceptance, and the church—which seemed so cold and detached.

"I was so torn emotionally about what to do. I wasn't able to make the decision immediately," Jane shared with me recently. "Fortunately, my husband was wise enough to give me the space and the time that I needed to make that decision. Mike also sought counsel and was told that I needed time and that he needed to give me that time. Consequently, it gave me freedom to work through my feelings without any pressure from him or the woman I had been involved with.

"I did not believe that I could change or that there was a way out of homosexuality," she said. "I had been told again and again by my gay friends that I had been born gay and I had come to believe those words." So with all the confusion, Jane cried out to God for help, "Lord Jesus...I have made a mess of my life. Please help me!"

Within days of the confrontation, her husband stopped by a Christian bookstore and picked up a personal testimony of overcoming homosexuality. Jane shared with me that she devoured the book in one sitting. That is how she found out about Exodus.

Jane attended an Exodus conference, where she experienced profound worship and heard personal stories that gave her hope for change. Much more significant was hearing the conclusion of 1 Corinthians 6:9-11. Jane had read and heard that those who practice homosexuality "will not inherit the kingdom of God" (1 Corinthians 6:10) but had never noticed verse 11, which read, "And that is what some of you were. But you were washed, you were sanctified, you were justified in the name of the Lord Jesus Christ and by the Spirit of our God." Jane's conclusion was, "Yes, change was possible. It no longer mattered what secular research claimed. Jesus had clearly said that I could be set free!"

Also, Jane had a powerful experience at the conference:

> During a prayer time at the conference, with the
> "eyes of my heart," I saw a picture. I was three
> years old, standing a few feet away from Jesus. His

arms were outstretched, his eyes radiated love. Then he picked me up and held me. At that moment the love of Jesus came pouring into my heart, filling it up to overflowing.

I realized right then and there that lesbian love was a counterfeit. It had never filled and never satisfied the deepest needs of my heart. But now I had found Jesus. He was a man I could trust, someone whose love truly fills and satisfies.

I didn't hesitate. At last I knew the truth. In my heart I closed the door once and for all to homosexuality. I struggled for awhile, but I never looked back.[15]

Mike's response was measured and required rebuilding trust with Jane. So the process that she went through over the following years progressed more rapidly than the one that Mike went through.

"He needed the time to work through the anger and to learn to trust me again," Jane explained. "Mike was extremely guarded and closed to me for some time. So when I was ready to work on building our marriage, I now needed to wait for him to work through his feelings. Only when he was able to let go of his anger and offer forgiveness were we able to come into a mutual marriage relationship."

Jane felt it took about a year to come to the point of rebuilding their marriage. "And now, it's as if that episode of my life never happened. It's so remote, 15 years later. Now, I can be so completely free and vulnerable with my husband that our marital intimacy just keeps getting better and better, including our sexual intimacy. It is beautiful to be experiencing marriage together the way God really meant it to be."

God places a very high value on marriage. It's not to be entered into lightly—either by straight couples or those who have left homosexuality. Any man or woman who has had a homosexual past will need to prayerfully consider many things before deciding on marriage. My best advice for you as a woman on the journey to wholeness is to let God have time to work His will in you. Don't hurry things along. God's timetable may have many surprises in store. Let Him, not you, be in charge of your future relationships with men.

10

Parenthood and the Ex-Gay Woman

John and I are privileged to know a number of men and women who left homosexuality and eventually married. Many have also raised healthy and secure children. Some of these couples have become our long-distance friends; others are closer in proximity. We are blessed with the opportunity to discuss parenting concerns with each other.

Sons are a heritage from the LORD, children a reward from Him (Psalm 127:3).

Many of these couples have courageously faced their pasts, matured, and moved on before committing to marriage and starting families. Others have begun to deal with their homosexuality after becoming married and having children. They didn't have the opportunity to mend their lives before, so they had to do some repair work afterward. Still other parents are just beginning this journey of facing and working through their past.

No matter where you fit into these scenarios, I encourage you to stay on the path toward change. In doing so, you will gain healthier perspectives and attitudes, which will naturally filter down to nourish the souls of your children. Many who are working through same-sex attraction are motivated to create a healthier environment for their children, and they experience significant healing more quickly.

Much of my practical advice in the pages that follow is based on personal conversations as well as key developmental theories concerning sexual orientation. For illustrations, I will draw upon my relationships with families with at least one ex-gay parent.

For readers who doubt they will ever be mothers—please read this chapter anyway. As we look at the roles of parents in the life of a child, you will likely see another missing piece in the puzzle of your own upbringing. And sometimes understanding what happened to us as our gender identity was formed can help us move past some of the resulting problems into a healthier identity.

The Importance of Mothering

Few will argue that mothers are vitally important to the well-being of their children—both sons and daughters. We women can best model connection and nurturing for our children from the beginning of their fragile lives. We are meant to completely engage with our infants, enjoying their steady gaze when they are first born and later reading books to them and listening sympathetically to their troubles at school. We, as mothers, are meant to provide a warm environment in which to care for our children.

As Dr. Brenda Hunter asks in her book *In the Company of Women*, "Why is maternal love so foundational that some women spend much of their adult lives either basking in its richness or working to understand why their mothers couldn't love them?"[1]

As a mother myself, I continue to marvel at the incredible bond I shared with my boys from the moment they were born. After each birth (by Caesarean section), my husband brought my sweet little boys to me where I could see, touch, and kiss them. All I could move was my head, but my maternal feelings for them swept me away. Tears of deep joy flowed down my face. I couldn't take my eyes off them. Oh, yes, I had fallen in love.

Not only does a mother fall in love with her baby, but our infants fall in love with us too. For months, while still in our womb, our son or daughter attached primarily to our voice. Dr. Hunter writes,

> We were born, then, programmed to fall in love with our mother. As babies we resonated to her smile; we picked up on her moods; we talked to her with our coos. If we were fortunate, she listened, held us close, cooed back, and established eye contact again and again. A lovely duet between a mother and her baby began.[2]

In *The Power of Mother Love,* Dr. Hunter concludes, "My years as a therapist have only underscored my conviction that our earliest bond with our mother is paramount, shaping all other intimate attachments as well as our sense of self."[3]

Unhealthy Gender Attitudes

Children are much more perceptive than we think. They pick up on subtle messages, such as the lie that men are "worthless" or women are "weak." Our children read our attitudes and hear our unspoken messages. Unfortunately some of us have lived with errant thoughts for so long that we don't even recognize what we're communicating in our homes.

Relating to Sons

For example, if a mother has a generalized resentment toward men—including their father—her children will respond to her attitudes. One child may absorb the message while another will discard or rebel against it. If a son absorbs the message that maleness is not good, he will not know what to think of his own developing masculinity and may later turn to gay relationships to solve his identity problems. His homosexuality is a natural result of taking in the message that masculinity is bad, rejecting that part of himself, and later needing to connect with his maleness.

Generalized resentment or hatred of men can lead to other responses from children as well. Perhaps the son rejects his mother's view of men. He may set about to show his disapproval through rebellion. After all, she is not creating an environment where he can feel good about his maleness. The result will probably be a strained relationship between mother and son.

Several families with grown children have realized that these dynamics were in action when their sons were younger. One mother shared with me, "I never realized the impact my attitudes toward men could have on my sons. Now my oldest son is reacting by proving his masculinity with an extra dose of machismo, and my youngest son is gay. Here I am at the age of 43, resolving my same-sex attractions and bad attitudes toward men," she told me, "and my sons are living out a painful search for their masculine identities. It grieves me to know that I contributed to that."

Relating to Daughters

What about ex-gay mothers who still experience unresolved disconnectedness from their own gender? This can be extremely problematic for daughters. The mother may not be emotionally available to her little girl, she may not be nurturing to the daughter, and/or she may not approve of her daughter's femininity. All of these outcomes derive from not having faced the past and can have devastating consequences on a little girl.

By using our mother as a mirror, we know what it is to be female (Brenda Hunter).[4]

Even if an ex-gay mother has been able to "be there" for her daughter emotionally, the mother may find certain expressions of her daughter's femininity difficult. For example, Jane Boyer told me, "My daughter wanted me to curl her hair, help her learn how to cook, and shop for clothes with her. I am not an expert on hairstyling or cooking, and shopping is certainly not my chosen pastime. Those sorts of things were very challenging for me."

For many women working through same-sex attraction, we've learned that our masculine attributes were overdeveloped and the feminine underdeveloped during our childhood years. Because of this dynamic, relating to a daughter may prove more challenging than to a son. We may easily connect with our sons' competitiveness and interest in athletics but struggle to sit down and do craft projects with our daughters. Each mother can choose to be stretched in these areas, connect with her daughter in feminine activities, and grow in healing because of her relationship with her child.

Girls desire to feel valued by their parents and want to remain emotionally and relationally connected to them. But instead of experiencing this connectedness, which she needs so desperately from birth on, the daughter of a gender-confused mother is likely to encounter emotional distance and detachment from her mother. If this cycle continues unaddressed, the daughter may suffer for the rest of her life, wondering about her worth and why her mother had a difficult time loving her.

Shelley, a woman I met in the Midwest, had just left a lesbian relationship two years before and had returned to her husband and family. She spoke with me about the problems in her relationship with her daughter.

> Anne, I married young because it was just the thing to do. I wasn't in love with my husband. I was trying to cover up my insecurity as an individual. Then, my first child was born—a little girl

named Amanda. I really didn't know how to relate to her. I couldn't seem to attach to her. She seemed too close, too much like me, and I couldn't deal with it. So I kept my emotional distance. Thank God that my husband could connect emotionally with her.

Now that Amanda is 11, we are dealing with the consequences of my emotional absence for a couple of years while I was completely invested in my ex-lover. I know my daughter's emotional outbursts and distance now are related to the fact that I haven't been there for her.

Not only does motherhood change us and make us more vulnerable emotionally, but as Dr. Brenda Hunter explains,

Pregnancy and new motherhood take a woman *home*. Home to her first intimate relationship. Home to her parents' marriage. Home to her earliest feelings of vulnerability and dependency...If you were loved, you can embrace motherhood because you wholeheartedly remember what it felt like to be held in the loving arms and gaze of your mother. You long to pass this rich legacy on.[5]

On the other hand, Dr. Hunter says, "A woman's past matters as she faces impending motherhood. It matters greatly whether she had a positive or negative nurturing history, for this is the part of the well she will draw from to nurture her baby."[6]

Motivation to Deal with the Past

Keep in mind that whatever you experienced as a child will show up in your own parenting unless you deal with it honestly. Consider the woman who was disciplined in anger or physically abused as a child. Unless she deliberately establishes new patterns, she may very well continue these negative patterns with her own children.

To provide a healthy environment for both sons and daughters, we mothers must examine how we feel about ourselves as women and what we believe about men. If we're not able to see the goodness of both sexes, we will not be able to provide a healthy environment in which our precious little ones can grow into healthy men and women. We can only give what we ourselves have attained. But if we face the challenge of dealing with our pasts, we will be personally rewarded, and we will give the gift of wholeness to our children.

> *It's always possible for a determined, thoughtful mother to find healing for her wounds and pass on more love and security to her children than she experienced during a childhood of privation or suffering (Brenda Hunter, Ph.D.).*[7]

Specific Parenting Skills

In chapter 4, I addressed the topic of healthy female gender development, so for a thorough review you may wish to revisit that chapter, reading with the perspective of a parent. Here I would like to guide and strengthen your relationships with your children—particularly young children. We will consider touch, words of affection, boundaries related to nudity, building up your spouse in front of the children, and encouraging the relationship with the same-gender parent.

Discipline and training children is an important subject, and others have written extensively on it. Books that I've found particularly useful include *Shepherding a Child's Heart* by Tedd Tripp, *Dare to Discipline* by Dr. James Dobson, and *She Calls Me Daddy* by Robert Wolgemuth. To their advice, I will simply add that discipline is to be used for training children. As parents, we are to take the leadership role of training our children by modeling godly behavior first, setting up parameters ahead of time, and then consistently following through with reasonable consequences. The consequences should never be administered in anger but out of love and with the goal of providing healthy limits and direction for our children.

Comforting and nurturing our children is also very important. If your child is crying and wants you to hug him or her, don't withhold your affection. Comforting a child is probably the best possible use of a human's arms. If your child is afraid, don't discount his or her fears but talk about the reality of the situation and comfort your child with both your words and your arms. Sacrifice whatever task you are doing, come down to your child's level, and offer your undistracted attention.

The Value of Touch

From birth, babies need to be held, cared for, and caressed. They thrive on eye contact with their parents and other close friends and family members. Touch is essential for their survival, as Neil and Briar Whitehead report in their book, *My Genes Made Me Do It!* The authors cite a thirteenth-century report of Frederick II of Germany's horrifying attempt to study language development. This dictator took infants from their homes and families and had nurses attend them only for feeding or bathing. "There was to be no cuddling, caressing, or speaking. The children did not survive long enough to develop any language at all. They all died."[8]

Touch is crucial for the well-being of sons and daughters, but touch should not be forced. I am sensitive to my sons even in the area of tickling. After a brief moment, I stop and if they wish to continue the game, they ask me to continue. Our boys love to be carried on their parents' shoulders, to wrestle with dad on the lawn, or to cuddle up next to one of us while we watch TV. I have so many wonderful memories with them, even though all three are still young boys, that I can't help but smile and look eagerly ahead for all the good times we have yet to share as a family.

Robert Wolgemuth comments on touch as a love language for daughters. "To your daughter, touching is the key to her heart."[9] A hug, a kiss on the cheek, stroking her hair, you name it—appropriate touch always says "I love you" and "You are precious to me."

The Value of Affectionate Words

Both boys and girls need to hear words of love and affection from their mom and dad. They need to know that you notice what they are good at, that you speak well of their gender, and that despite imperfect behavior, *you love them.*

My sons are currently at the ages when they like to race, jump, and play hard. They are testing themselves against their friends' abilities and interests. When Timmy, my six-year-old, tells me about a superhero game he played with friends at school, I respond with enthusiasm. "Wow, that sounds cool, Timmy. Which superhero were you?" With two brief comments, I just affirmed his maleness and his interests.

Wolgemuth describes your words of affection to your daughters. "'Touching words'—statements of affection—are the agreement that physical touch seals. They define exactly what it is you're thinking or feeling. They leave no room for doubt."[10]

At bedtime when we're finished reading a book, my husband or I will share a story about how much each of our boys mean to us. The boys listen quietly and intently as we talk about the funny little things they used to do as babies and how much we love them. I can't read certain books to them without crying, such as *Guess How Much I Love You* by Sam McBratney. And then I have to explain why I'm crying. I sure am a softy now—I wasn't always that way.

We all know that words can either build up or break down. We must be very careful with what proceeds from our mouths. If you find yourself demeaning your children with words, calling names, or constantly criticizing them, please get immediate help. You may wish to get direction from a pastor or Christian counselor, but *get help*. For as Scripture says, "Reckless words pierce like a sword, but the tongue of the wise brings healing" (Proverbs 12:18).

Issues with Nudity

At a very young age, seeing Mom or Dad without clothes is really a nonissue. In fact, from birth to age two, you will have to leave the bathroom door open or bring your child in with you. Otherwise, havoc or danger could hit like a tornado.

Even at age three, most children really don't notice their parent's body or experience any form of embarrassment. When they start to notice the opposite-gender parent's body is when that parent should no longer allow them to see her/him in the shower or changing clothes. According to my experience, that starts to happen when children are between three and four years old. Modesty kicks in about that time also. It's okay if a boy continues to take a shower with his dad—after all, Daddy is just like him. But it's about that time that the opposite-gender parent's body should begin to become mysterious. The boundaries go up in the area of nudity.

As a mother, I still give my sons baths, but I also respect their modesty. If they wish, I will turn my head until they are covered up in the bubble bath. I still need to be there to make sure they are safe and wash their hair. Likewise, my six-year-old son knows to respect me by not coming into my bathroom when I am showering or changing.

Dr. Stanton Jones, coauthor of *Homosexuality: The Use of Scientific Research in the Church's Moral Debate*, reports a key theory that Daryl Bem, professor of psychology at Cornell University in New York, has developed called the "Exotic Becomes Erotic" theory. Bem suggests that "individuals can become erotically attracted to classes of individuals from whom they felt different during childhood."[11] Dr. Jones writes, "Bem suggests that being raised to be most familiar with your same-sex group results in a certain mysteriousness or 'exoticness' of the other sex, and what is exotic tends to be regarded as sexually attractive or 'erotic' in adult life."[12]

The female body should become "mysterious" to our sons and the male body mysterious to our daughters. By the time our opposite-sex children are the age of four, we should no longer be nude in their presence. Instead, they should identify with the same-gender parent's body.

Building Up Your Spouse

Children receive great benefit when their father and mother demonstrate their respect for each other. Children need to see their mother honor their father verbally and otherwise. Likewise, they need to see their father expressing his love for his wife with words and actions. When children see respect, honor, and affection between their parents, they learn how a marriage is to function—how a man should treat his wife and how a wife should respond lovingly to her husband.

We read in the New Testament,

> Husbands, love your wives, just as Christ loved the church and gave himself up for her to make her holy, cleansing her by the washing with water through the word, and to present her to himself as a radiant church, without stain or wrinkle or any other blemish, but holy and blameless. In this same way, husbands ought to love their wives as their own bodies. He who loves his wife loves himself (Ephesians 5:25-28).

That is a pretty big order for men to fill!

To the wife, Scripture says, "Wives, submit to your husbands as to the Lord," and "the wife must respect her husband" (Ephesians 5:22-33). If the word "femininity" has implied weakness for some of us women, how much more does "submission" sound dissonant in our ears! But we must understand that in biblical usage, *submission* does not mean "lesser than." It simply implies an order of command. If no one submitted to a general in an army, the army could not function. Men submit to a chain of command at work, in the military, as well as at church—without thinking twice about it. Even the Vice President submits to the President of the United States. You, as a wife, are the vice president of your family. Just keep in mind that *submission* does not equate with "lesser" but describes an order of authority.

Encouraging the Child's Relationship with the Same-Sex Parent

We mothers need to encourage the relationship between father and son and not intercept their communications. Our sons need to relate directly to and identify with their father.

> *Attachment implies sameness. "I love my mother and want to grow up to be just like her" is the hallmark of the identification processes in the little girl (Dr. Brenda Hunter).*[13]

Women can easily step in because of our intuitive nature—but that is not appropriate.

Let me give you a personal example. I was putting away laundry in my son's room when he turned to me and said, "Mom, I'm mad at Dad."

"Oh really Timmy, what's the matter?" I asked.

To be honest, I cannot remember what the complaint was, but realizing that he was serious, I responded, "Well, why don't you go talk to your dad about it?" Timmy followed my advice and walked downstairs to talk with his dad. Within minutes, the problem was resolved and they were bonded together even more.

The same goes for the mother-daughter relationship. Fathers should encourage the daughters and their mother to connect or reconnect, unless they have an unhealthy relationship. If the mother has untreated psychological problems, such as bipolar disorder, or is constantly critical of her daughter, this might be more harmful than helpful to the daughter. Assuming hope exists for a healthy relationship between the two, the father should encourage bonding and step out of their developing intimacy.

Your children also need to have good, nurturing relationships with the opposite-gender parent, as discussed extensively in chapter 4.

Extended Family Relationships

When talking with other ex-gay parents, I am sometimes surprised by their stories about their extended family members who are having trouble in child-rearing. One friend shared:

> Although I have dealt with "my stuff" and moved on, my straight sister did not go for counseling about our upbringing. She always used to say that "Homosexuality is your issue, not mine. What do I need counseling for?"
>
> Well, my children are doing very well, but my sister's children are struggling with their gender identity. I can see it from afar. And, what's worse, I can see her duplicating my mother's criticism of men and over-dependence on her children. It's actually scary. If those kids don't end up gay, it will be a miracle!

I have heard this so many times that I am no longer surprised by it. If siblings are unwilling to face up to the difficulties in their life, to forgive and to work through a similar process of healing childhood wounds as their same-sex attracted brother or sister, they will likely duplicate the faulty parenting they received. Denial doesn't shield us from the repercussions of the original family environment.

Instead, faulty family dynamics are duplicated through generations unless they are confronted deliberately. As many Christian parents say, "This is our opportunity to stop unhealthy patterns for the next generation. These things do not have to continue on. I have the opportunity and responsibility to change for the sake of my children."

Oh, if only our extended families felt so strongly!

Passing On a New Heritage

Even if you have not worked on resolving your past and your family-of-origin dynamics before having children, you still have time to repair any damage you may have passed down to your children. Humility and forgiveness can be powerful help in healing wounds. You need to work through your own childhood issues, and so do your children. This begins the process of handing down a new heritage to them.

As mothers, we have to realize that our nurture is incredibly valuable and will impact the rest of our children's lives—especially their ability to bond with loved ones. The mother-child relationship is the first significant intimate relationship that humans experience, and it shapes all others that follow. We must work through the problems in our own past so our children will receive the nurture from us they so desperately need.

We parents need to be aware of the residual attitudes that fester from our past beliefs. If we communicate that men are bad or women are weak, we will naturally affect our children's perceptions of themselves. Instead we should carefully evaluate what we are communicating about gender to our children and correct ourselves when necessary. Fortunately for us and our children, God is in the business of binding up the brokenhearted and healing their wounds (Psalm 147:3). Someone greater than us is willing to fight beside us in the battle for health and wholeness. As His Word promises,

> He has sent me to bind up the brokenhearted, to proclaim freedom for the captives and release from darkness for the prisoners, to proclaim the year of the Lord's favor and the day of vengeance of our God, to comfort all who mourn, and to provide for those who grieve in Zion—to bestow on them a crown of beauty instead of ashes, the oil of gladness instead of mourning, and a garment of praise instead of a spirit of despair (Isaiah 61:1-3).

Our True Goal

A woman who has abandoned her lesbianism will discover that God offers her a life of fullness. That life may or may not include a husband and children. But it *always* will include God's best design for that particular woman.

My advice, then, is not to seek a husband—nor necessarily a romantic relationship with a man. Rather, wait and see what God has to offer. Be ready for remaining single, but also be ready for a special man if that's God's choice for you.

Similarly, your future may or may not include motherhood. Be content if God says yes or if He says no. Our goal must always be to receive God's best. As evangelist Dwight Moody advised more than a hundred years ago: "Spread out your petition before God, and then say, 'Thy will, not mine be done.' The sweetest lesson I have learned in God's school is to let the Lord choose for me."

As you move into wholeness as a woman, make that your motto. You will never regret it.

_As_ _We_ _P_art

Blessed are those whose strength is in you, who have set their hearts on pilgrimage. As they pass through the Valley of Baca (or weeping), they make it a place of springs; the autumn rains also cover it with pools. They go from strength to strength, till each appears before God in Zion." (Psalm 84:5-7)

At the beginning of this book, I likened coming out of homosexuality to a journey. I mentioned that the road will have its ups and downs, its curves, and thankfully, its nice straight highways where you can speed along with relative ease.

In a few more pages, you will close the covers of this book. I hope that you have found answers and encouragement in its pages and will refer to it as ofen as you feel necessary. At the same time, I realize that your story is unique, and the many twists and turns ahead of you will hold choices for you to make along the way. What you decide at each juncture will determine your own individual pathway. If you have surrended your life to Jesus Christ, you will have a ready compainion along the way "Whether you turn to the right or to the left, your ears will hear a voice behind you, saying, 'This is the way; walk in it" (Isaiah 30:21). It is up to you to listen and move forward into wholeness.

The Ex-Gay Plateau

If you are like most woman overcoming homosexual attraction and identity, you may come to a place of resst along the way and feel reluctant to get up and move on. After facing pain and change, we do need rest. But eventually, we must continue our trek to gain all that awaits us. Remaining in an incomplete identity has been called the "ex-gay plateau" by Sy Rogers, a popular spokesman in the ex-gay community.

For most of us, the process of embracing our God-given female identities and then stepping outward into the lives of others is the way off the ex-gay plateau. I have been helped over the years by learning that I am not significantly different from other women around me. Neither are you. The difference usually lies in the outward expression of how we have dealt with our insecurities, fears, and wounds, rather than in our natures as women.

In chapter 7, I quoted a young lady named Sydney who told me, "I used to get so hung up on the same-sex attraction element, when really what was at the core of my sin had little to do with sex. It has become abundantly evident to me that many women are seeking to find their sufficiency in someone or something else, other than God. I am not alone."

My hope is that you feel similarly to Sydney—that you are not alone in your situation or struggles. My hope is that you may begin to see the similarities between yourself and other women who have not dealt with same-sex attraction.

Closing the Back Door

One sure way to avoid getting stuck in the process of change is to shut the back door—to remove forever your option to return to lesbian relationships, identity, or culture.

One of my pastors used to say, "Board up the windows and brick over the old door. Commit to not return to the past."

To apply this principle, simply ask God to give you an undivided heart devoted to His ways, commit in prayer to not returning to your past, and ask Him to give you a hatred for your sin.

That last suggestion was quite profound in my life. I had been working on my same-sex attraction issues for a couple of years when I ventured to ask God to give me a hatred for my sin. As a result of that prayer, I began to see homosexuality and homosexual relationships in a whole new light. Instead of my typical attraction to women who appeared to be lesbians, I found myself experiencing a new and profound sadness. I didn't feel judgmental, harsh, or angry. Rather, I felt sad. I think God was giving me a glimpse of the destructiveness of sin.

For example, I remember going to a softball tournament to cheer on a friend. While watching the game, I noticed several lesbians and expected to feel attraction toward them. Instead, I noticed the pain underneath their defensive exteriors. I realized by looking at some of the women that they had deeply rejected their own value as women, probably because of painful past experiences. I had eyes that could look beyond the exterior into their hearts. The experience impacted me deeply.

On the other hand, we could assume that the past is gone from our memories forever and that we could not possibly return to the old ways. I consider this foolishness because we still carry around with us a sinful nature (Psalm 51:5; Romans 8:12-14) that will be eliminated forever when we enter eternity (Revelation 22:3-5,14). Until then, my human fallibility remains part of me and ever in need of the lordship of Jesus Christ and the daily leadership of the Holy Spirit (Romans 8:5-9, Hebrews 12:1-3).

> *He who is full loathes honey, but to the hungry even what is bitter tastes sweet (Proverbs 27:7).*

I realize that if same-sex temptation happens to occur, I have the tools, the understanding, and the relationship with God to overcome any temptation. We *always* have a way out of any temptation (1 Corinthians 10:13). Also, I do not intend to be ashamed if I'm tempted, for temptation is not sin. I have the choice of how to respond to the temptation. The old solutions used to taste sweet, but not anymore—they are bitter and unfruitful offerings.

Finally, please know that the Body of Christ is in need of women (and men) today who are transparent and able to use their pasts to help others. The church in general can benefit from the life lessons you learn and apply. My hope is that you will make this one of your goals. Many women still struggle daily with the issues you will already have resolved. You can help them by being part of a local support group, offering financial and voluntary assistance to ministries that help women struggling with homosexuality move into a new life, and most important, praying for these ministries and the women who seek help through them.

God bless you in your journey.

> May God himself, the God of peace, sanctify you through and through. May your whole spirit, soul and body be kept blameless at the coming of our Lord Jesus Christ. The one who calls you is faithful and he will do it (1 Thessalonians 5:23-24).

Appendix A: Frequently Asked Questions

*B*ecause of my personal experience with lesbianism and the nature of the ministry in which I'm involved, I'm often asked certain basic questions. Here are some of those "frequently asked questions" with brief answers. If the subject is more fully addressed in the chapters of *Restoring Sexual Identity,* I mention the chapters in which that topic is discussed.

Are men and women with homosexual feelings "born gay"?

Popular media promote the thought that men and women are born homosexual, but the research simply does not back up that claim. A stronger argument favors the influence of a number of factors: sexual abuse in childhood, internal conclusions about the value and worth of the person's gender, and the gender of the parent the individual modeled as a child. This topic is covered more fully in chapters 2 and 3.

Can a woman really change her sexual orientation?

Change certainly can occur. In fact, therapist Steven Donaldson asserts that changing a person's sexual orientation may be easier than overcoming drug or alcohol addiction. In my life and the lives of the 265 women who filled out my survey, the first major change was a new appreciation of womanhood. That initial change helped bring about heterosexual identification. For more information, you may wish to read chapter 5.

Will I ever stop being tempted with sexual feelings toward another woman?

Often when we begin to deal with the issues underlying same-sex attraction, homosexual feelings may seem a bit stronger. But as we face challenges that may seem unrelated to our temptations, our same-sex attraction lessens and eventually takes a back seat to other struggles and concerns in our lives.

In 1987 when I began to face problems in a deliberate manner, I found myself struggling with lesbian thoughts on a daily basis. But now, 16 years later, as a wife and mother, I find such thoughts a rarity. This topic is thoroughly covered in chapter 7, and more examples from my life are in my husband's and my autobiography, *Love Won Out*.

My friend at work is a lesbian. She says she is happy, but I would like to talk to her about her life. What should I do?

First, remember that homosexuality at its root is not sexual. Instead it's an ineffective coping mechanism—a false way to love and nurture oneself. At the base of homosexual attraction is a disconnect with a woman's sense and enjoyment of being a female. She may look happy to the outside world, but at quiet moments she most likely experiences feelings of unfulfillment.

What she needs more than anything is a relationship with Jesus Christ and the nurture that comes from God alone. Pray that she may know the comfort and peace that surpasses understanding.

God is the one who will give her understanding that lesbian relationships are "missing the mark" and that they are not His desire or design for her.

My coworker says she is a Christian and a lesbian. She even attends church regularly. I'm confused—can a person be both?

She may very well be a Christian—only God can judge her heart. People have developed many arguments using various Scriptures to justify homosexual behavior. Believe it or not, some people teach a so-called "gay theology," but this a revisionist view of Scripture. In other words, if she is claiming that the Bible says lesbianism is acceptable, she must have reinterpreted Scripture to fit her feelings.

The easiest way to evaluate the claims of "gay theology" is to see if anywhere in Scripture God endorses sexuality outside the boundaries of marriage between a woman and a man. Nowhere does Scripture endorse sexual expression between two women or two men. For more information, read Joe Dallas' book, *A Strong Delusion: Confronting the "Gay Christian" Movement* (Harvest House Publishers, 1996).

My daughter has just told me she's gay, and I'm feeling overwhelming grief. What can I do?

Many parents grieve deeply when they find out about their child's homosexuality. They face letting go of their dreams of their daughter's heterosexual marriage and natural children. They may wonder how they could have not known their daughter well enough to have perceived her struggle. And they may feel that their daughter is rejecting their marriage.

These feelings can be very powerful. I would encourage you to find support from parents who have survived their child's admission of same-sex attraction. Some of these parents have not only survived but actually become stronger individuals. The Exodus office can refer you to a ministry that cares for parents of homosexually attracted children. I also recommend making an appointment to speak with your pastor or priest and eventually risk talking with your closest friends about it. You are in great need of support and understanding at this time.

As a parent, I'm wondering what I did wrong. Am I responsible for my daughter's homosexuality?

No one is responsible for another person's actions or feelings. But if you read chapters 3 and 4 and find that you contributed to her struggles in any way, you can always take the powerful step of saying, "I'm sorry."

It's also important to keep in mind that your daughter's perceptions of circumstances and decisions based on her experiences played a huge part in the development of same-sex deficit and attraction. It may be wise to ask her views and feelings about life when growing up. If you decide to do this, be prepared to listen without defensiveness and you will be openings a very significant door of communication with your daughter. May the Lord bless you as you seek understanding and a heart-to-heart relationship with her.

Where can I find additional resources?

In chapter 5, I mentioned several resources for support. For written materials, I recommend contacting Exodus at (888) 264-0877 or www.exodus-international.org and asking for a book list. I've also suggested a list of additional resources on page 259.

Appendix B:
Survey Results

The following survey was not done in an academic setting and is not a scientific research project. It does, however, reflect the hearts of the women who participated in it. The background information these women so generously provided in their responses offers insight, encouragement, affirmation, and direction to all of us who have struggled with same-sex attractions.

In April, 1999, I came up with the idea of surveying women who are overcoming or who have overcome homosexuality. The main purpose of the research was to provide data for *Restoring Sexual Identity.* I felt that the study was important for a number of reasons. Quantitative data on the experiences and backgrounds of same-sex attracted women is lacking. I desired to test some of the theories on the development of lesbianism. And finally, I believed that women interested in overcoming lesbianism would be interested in responding to such a survey and in seeing how others' experience coincided with or differed from their own.

My intent was to query women within Exodus International, an organized network of ministries assisting men and women leaving homosexuality. I also intended to have a smaller control group of approximately 40 to 50 lesbian-identified women.

The Process of Development

In September, 1999, I drafted my initial two-page list of questions. From then through March, 2000, I obtained content review and development help from 11 experts in the Christian ex-gay movement, as well as three additional experts in other areas. The reviewers included Bob Davies (former Executive Director for Exodus International), five national women's leaders within Exodus, and three professional therapists. By the end of March, 2000, I had developed a list of 142 questions. By the final development in May, 2000, the survey was eight pages.

Along the way, several people contributed their expertise and insight in the area of design review. In particular, Katy Vorce assisted in minimizing question bias, restructuring the order of questions, and reviewing the wording for clarity and consistency. She provided invaluable help in this area on three such revisions. John McKeever advised me about the distribution of the survey.

I sent a final copy to each of my reviewers and asked them to look for duplicate questions, flow of questions, questions in the wrong sections, unclear meanings of terms or questions, and questions that could easily be interpreted in two or more ways.

In June, 2000, I distributed 1884 surveys through Exodus referral ministries, predominately in the United States and Canada. An Exodus affiliate in Singapore was also interested and distributed 11 surveys.

In addition, I announced the survey on Focus on the Family's *Renewing the Heart* and Janet Parshall's *America* radio programs. I received 28 individual requests for surveys as a result. Additionally in August, 2000, I distributed 150 surveys at the Exodus North America Annual Conference.

In the end, I distributed 1912 surveys. Of these, 265 were filled out and returned to me by March, 2001 (a return rate of 14%). The lesbian survey fared better in the percentage of returns (32%), but the small number returned (nine) was inadequate for a control group.

General Demographics

Of the 265 same-sex attracted women who filled out the survey, more than two-thirds were between the ages of 25 and 45. Slightly more than 8% were younger than 25. Almost 20% were 45 years of age and older.

Of those who responded, 83% were Caucasian, 5% were African American, 4% were Asian, 5% were Latino/Hispanic, and 3% described themselves as "other."

A little more than 2% of the women were hearing impaired. Almost 55% listed an annual income between $20,000 and $50,000, just over 25% of the women earned less than $20,000 annually and almost one out of six (16%) earned more than $50,000 annually.

A third had completed some college, another third had graduated from college, and 16% had achieved a master's degree or higher. Fourteen percent had attained only high school educations.

Nearly two-thirds of the women had never been married, just under a quarter were currently married, and roughly 10% were divorced or separated.

One-third of the women had invested between one and three years receiving help for their same-gender sexual attraction, while 15% had spent less than one year receiving help. Another 20% devoted four to seven years to receiving help, and the remaining nearly 20% spent eight or more years obtaining assistance.

A little over half of the women had received help through Exodus, half received additional help through professional therapy and more than one-third used other means, which included pastoral or lay counseling. About 43% used multiple means to achieve their goals. The most common combination was an Exodus ministry and a professional therapist (almost 20%).

Before help 57% of the women identified themselves as lesbians, 19% as bisexual, and the rest as heterosexual, "ex-lesbian" or "other." (see chart below).

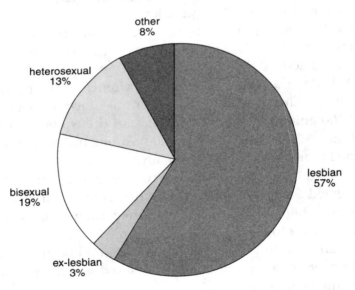

Sexual Identification Before Help

The women declared their sexual identification at the time of the survey as heterosexual (43%), ex-lesbian (one-third), lesbian (7%), bisexual (5%), and other (11%) (see chart on the next page).

Sexual Identification After Help

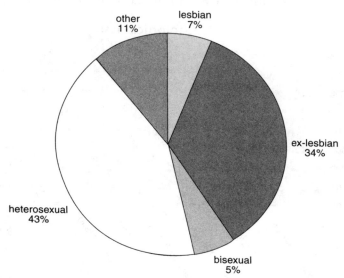

Of the 219 respondents who said they have experienced or been diagnosed with psychological issues, almost 40% had experienced one or two such issues at some point in time. Nearly 30% had experienced three or four psychological issues, and more than 14% experienced more than four psychological issues at some point in their lives. More than 17% expressed no psychological issues. The query included the following topics: depression, suicide attempts, drug use/chemical dependency, overeating, bulimia, anorexia, alcoholic behavior, self-mutilation, and other. These were the responses:

- depression—(67%)

- alcoholism—(38%)

- overeating—(31%)

- drug use/chemical dependency—(28%)

- suicide attempts—(25%)

- The least frequent psychological issues were self-mutilation (16%), anorexia (7%), and bulimia (7%).

Psychological Issues

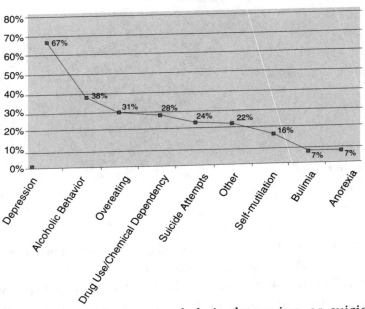

When asked the cause of their depression or suicide attempts, they answered,

- the breakup of a same-gender sexual or romantic relationship (61%)

- general despair (58%)

- hopelessness of real change (55%)

- clinical depression (34%)

- other (22%)

- pressure from others to change orientation (21%).

Not one respondent answered "pressure" as a singular answer. All other responses were at times answered as singular causes.

Parent/Family Relationships

Of the respondents, 7% were adopted as children and 4% were placed in foster care as children.

Just over half (57%) were brought up in an actively Christian home. In almost 30% of the families, the parents had divorced or separated before the respondent reached the age of 18. If the parents were divorced, the vast majority (93%) lived with their mother.

Almost 40% of the women grew up in households where one parent was an alcoholic. The parent abusing alcohol was the father in 30% of the cases, then the mother (7%), followed by the step-father (4%). Some families had more than one parent abusing alcohol. Substance abuse by the parents was much lower—15%.

When asked who the female respondent felt closer to when growing up, 42% named the mother, one-quarter checked off "father" and 32% selected neither parent.

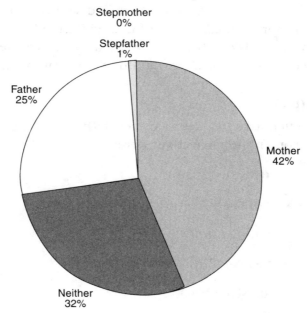

Closer Relationship

Mothers

In response to the question, "How did you view your mother when you were growing up?" the top four descriptions and their responses were:

- critical (49%)

- domineering (37%)

- detached (37%)

- weak (34%)

Sadly, few of the women were able to describe their mothers as:

- nurturing (23%)

- actively involved (22%)

- affirming (17%)

Almost one-third of those polled said their mother was absent for a critical period of their childhood.

When asked if they had wanted to be like their mother when growing up, an astounding 84% answered no.

Fathers

When asked to describe their fathers when growing up, the women's top adjectives were:

- detached (46%)

- critical (37%)

- strong (35%)

- passive (33%)

- abusive (28%)

Three out of the four positive views of their fathers fell to the bottom of the list:

- affirming (18%)

- nurturing (16%)

- actively involved (15%)

Even with these descriptions and closer relationships with their mothers, 75% of the women viewed the male gender as more desirable role models.

Other Family/Childhood Dynamics

Almost half of the respondents (46%) grew up hearing negative or degrading comments about women. Almost two-thirds (62%) of the reported comments originated from their fathers, while another one-third (35%) came from the girl's brothers (35%) and one-quarter (27%) from the mothers.

Abuse

These are the definitions of abuse in the survey:

- *verbal abuse*—calling a child insulting names or almost constant words of anger regardless of the child's behavior

- *emotional abuse*—words of manipulation, such as blaming the child for the adult's problems, regretting the child's birth, controlling through guilt or shame, and using the child as spousal emotional support

- *physical abuse*—physical injury of substantial harm or genuine threat of substantial harm by a parent or caregiver (excluding accidents)

- *neglect*—the failure to provide the basics of food, clothing, shelter, and appropriate supervision, as well as the failure to remove a child from a situation where she is exposed to abuse

- *abandonment*—the lack of emotional or physical presence or leaving the child without supervision

- *spiritual abuse*—the misdirected spiritual authority or coercion over another person's life

- *sexual molestation*—includes any kind of sexual interchange between a child and anyone bigger, stronger, or older, from inappropriate touching to kissing, contact with another's genitals, contact with the child's genitals, also includes exposure to another's genitals, exposure to pornographic materials, or use of child to make pornographic materials (may or may not include vaginal, oral, or anal intercourse)

An astounding 91% of the women had experienced some form of abuse when growing up. The abuses cited most often were emotional abuse (69%), followed closely by sexual abuse (66%) and verbal abuse (53%) (see chapter 6 for the information illustrated in chart form).

Almost two-thirds (62%) of the women reported witnessing the abuse of a family member. Predominately witnessed abuses were verbal (72%), emotional (72%), and physical abuse (57%), and abandonment (26%), yet in 10% of those cases, the child witnessed sexual abuse perpetrated on a family member.

Three-fourths of the women who were victims of sexual abuse were first sexually molested between three and ten years of age (75%).

Age When First Sexually Molested

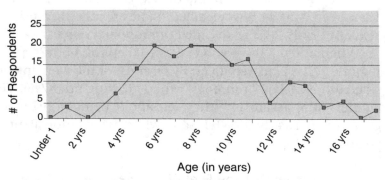

Age (in years)

Two-thirds of the respondents had been sexually molested by a male when under the age of 18. Of those molested, 85% were sexually molested by a male. The most common male perpetrator was reported as a male outside the family (58%), followed by "family friend" (24%), "other family member," which did not include father, brother or step-brother (23%), and then "brother" (23%).

Respondents reported molestation by a female in 17% of the cases. If molested by a female, the largest identifiable group of perpetrator was a babysitter (18%), followed by mother (14%), other family member (other than mother and sister) (11%), family friend (9%), and finally sister and church leader (5%). The largest group that was indicated as responsible for female-female sexual molestation was "other female"—anyone who did not fit into the other categories.

The majority of those molested by a female (89%) were molested by one individual. By contrast, if a girl was molested by a male, which happened to four times the number of women, she was more likely to also have been molested by a second male (24%).

Peer Relationships in Childhood

Although 60% of respondents experienced ridicule from their peers and 44% were called names related to gender or sexuality, only 22% were called homosexual names.

When asked, "Were you ever mistaken for a boy?" a firm majority (61%) answered yes. By far most of the women considered themselves "tomboys" when growing up (87%). The women were asked how they felt about being a girl when growing up. Nearly 90% felt somewhere from ambivalent to greatly disliking being a girl.

How Did You Feel About Being a Girl?

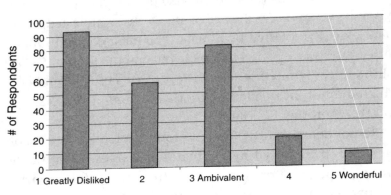

Just over 70% reported being more intrigued or captivated by girls than by boys during adolescence. Only one-third of the same-sex attracted women experimented with another girl sexually before the age of 13.

Opposite-Gender Experiences

This portion of survey results seem to confirm the fluidity of female sexuality.

As reported previously, nearly two-thirds of respondents (64%) identified themselves as lesbians before receiving help concerning same-sex attractions. Before the age of 18, more than half of the women (51%) hoped to get married to a loving man. Sixty percent had experienced feeling protected by a man. One-half (51%) stated they had an emotionally and sexually appealing dating relationship with a man, and almost three-fourths of the women said they'd had an intentional sexual experience with a man. Most of these women (61%) said they'd had this experience *after* their first same-gender sexual attraction. Three out of ten (32%) had deliberate sex with a man before ever experiencing sexual attraction to another woman.

Even so, a vast majority of the women (88%) said they had treated men in general with distrust or hostility. Perhaps having experienced sexual abuse in childhood (66%) by a male contributed to their distrust and hostility. Only 42% affirmed that they currently need men in their lives.

Same-Sex Attraction

By far, most of the respondents (83%) acknowledged "feeling different" from other girls or women. There was a significant correlation between "feeling different" and first experiencing same-sex attraction.*

Correlation Between First Feeling Different, First Same-Sex Attraction, and First Molestation

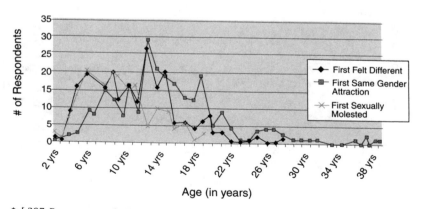

* [.387 Pearson correlation coefficient, significant at the 0.01 level (two-tailed)]
  Feeling different also correlated somewhat with the first incidence of sexual abuse.
  [.212 Pearson correlation coefficient, significant at the 0.05 level (two-tailed)]

A huge majority of the women (89%) had participated in a same-gender sexual experience. Additionally, 91% had had same-gender sexual fantasies. The top three forms of same-sex fantasy experienced were personal imagination (83%), movies (52%), visual pornography (41%), and lesbian novels or romance novels (31%). A majority (62%) had same-sex fantasies before the age of 18.

I asked the respondents, "Have you ever had an intensely emotional, exclusive relationship with another woman?" Again, most (93%) answered yes. Of those, 68% had up to six such relationships, while exactly half considered themselves heterosexual before the experience. Most (57%) said they had a personal relationship with Jesus Christ before engaging in a lesbian sexual experience. Additionally, nearly three-quarters of the women (74%) felt that their same-sex attractions were in conflict with their faith or conscience. What I find intriguing is the delay of a couple of years between same-sex attraction and experience (see chart below).

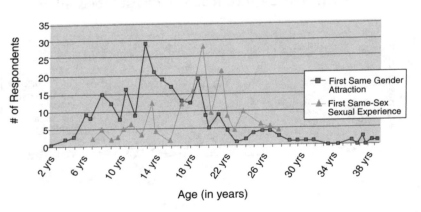

Correlation Between First Same-Sex Attraction and First Same-Gender Sexual Experience

Nearly a third (30%) of the women were initiated into a lesbian sexual experience by women who were three or more years older. Of these, 41% were seduced by someone in a "role of authority."

Forty percent of the respondents were seduced into their first lesbian sexual experience and in turn seduced other women into first lesbian experiences. Of those, 82% claimed that they had drawn up to two individuals into her first homosexual experience. Among the women who had a lesbian experience, three-fourths had had up to seven female sexual partners.

As far as length of lesbian relationships, three-fourths of the women (78%) claimed to have been in a long-term relationship, defined by 65% as "up to five years." The peak lengths of relationships were two and three years (32%).

Just over one-half (55%) acknowledged using emotional manipulation to maintain a lesbian relationship and a surprising one-third (36%) experienced a physically abusive episode with a female lover.

Marriage and Lesbian Involvement

Half (52%) of the married (or previously married) women had been sexually involved with another woman before getting married. One-third (35%) were involved sexually with another woman during their marriage, whereas 44% were involved following the breakup of their marriage. Some of the women were involved with other women sexually before, during, and after their marriages.

Nearly half of the married women (46%) experienced abuse by their spouse. The primary forms of difficulty were emotional neglect (68%) and emotional and verbal abuse (59% each). Nearly 20% left their husbands to get involved in a lesbian relationship. Much fewer (6%) left their children for a female lover.

Lesbian Experience/Culture

Nearly half of the women (47%) adopted the lesbian label, and the vast majority (77%) did so between ages 15 and 25. Once again, several years generally transpired between a woman first having same-sex attractions and eventually adopting a "lesbian" identity.

Correlation Between Same Gender Attraction and Adopting Lesbian Label

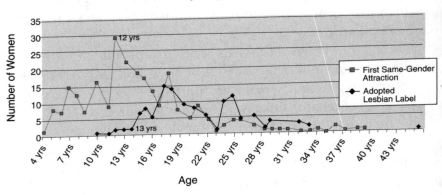

Two-thirds of the female respondents claimed involvement in the lesbian subculture. Sixty percent said they were barely to moderately involved. Another one-fourth were mostly involved, and 10% were completely immersed in the lesbian subculture. For those involved, lesbian or gay bars were the main outlet (86%); lesbian parties (62%), and adult women's sports (45%) were followed by feminist women's events (23%).

Of those involved in the lesbian subculture, 60% distanced themselves from non-homosexual friendships. More than a third (36%) had family members who lovingly reached out to them, despite not approving of their lesbian involvement. The good news is that 88% of these women said they have since reconciled with those family members. Among this group, the following situations were rare: registering with a female domestic partner (4%), commemorating a lesbian relationship with a religious commitment ceremony (7%), or using donor sperm to have a baby in a lesbian partnership (1%).

Pursuing Change

The top reason by far cited for pursuing change was "relationship with God" (95%). Feelings of shame (35%) and unhealthy lesbian partnerships (15%) followed as the second and third most common reasons to pursue change. Societal or family pressure was listed as a reason to pursue change by only 6% and 8% of the respondents respectively.

When asked how confident they were that they would change, the women responded that they were: very confident (58%), hopeful (31%), unsure (10%), or doubtful (2%). Hopeful and very confident comprised almost nine out of ten of the responses (89%).

The respondents claimed almost universally (98%) to have a personal relationship with Jesus Christ. Almost all (97%) said they believe homosexual behavior is sin and that they do not believe they were born homosexual, although 40% said they used to believe they were born gay.

When asked about the two most challenging aspects of overcoming lesbianism, they listed most frequently "loneliness" (55%) and "miss the sexual (or potential) intimacy with a woman" (44%). The next most common answers were "identity limbo" (24%), "fear of intimacy" (23%), "difficulty facing the past" (18%), and "fear of change" (13%). The least-mentioned challenges were "missing community" (9%) and dealing with the "born gay belief" (0.4%).

When asked, *What are the two most rewarding aspects of overcoming lesbianism?* the women answered first "presence of God" in their lives (79%) and "peace" (43%). Other answers included "hope for the future" (27%), "potential of marriage/family" (16%), "joy" (15%), "confidence" (11%), and "overcoming other difficulties more easily" (10%).

I asked if they had ever voiced or demonstrated attraction toward another lesbian struggler while pursuing sexual orientation change. I then asked those who responded yes if their overtures had been a precursor to a sexual experience with the woman. Half of the women admitted they had demonstrated attraction toward another woman struggling with lesbian attraction while pursuing change and one-third of those respondents confirmed a sexual experience following that disclosure. Overall, 18% became sexually involved with another female while working through the process of change.

Christian Involvement

Concerning their Christian involvement, almost all of the respondents (97%) said they attend a local church. When asked how frequently, one-half answered weekly (51%), and 43% reported attendance several times a week. In other words, these women are some of the most committed church members. Additionally, exactly two-thirds also attend a small group or are involved in a Bible study at their local churches.

Support System

Almost 60% said they have a support person at their local church. Of those, 90% have a female support person. The main settings that have helped to develop these relationships were listed as small group fellowship (40%), Bible study (18%), and church counselor (14%). The "other" encompassed an additional group of four out of ten experiences.

Challenges the women faced in maintaining a healthy female mentor relationship were listed as fear of rejection (39%), issues of trust (31%), feelings of vulnerability (27%), availability (25%), fear of attraction (18%), and fear of intimacy (14%).

Of those who did not have a female mentor, 82% desired such a relationship. The main challenges cited when finding a mentor included "haven't found the right person" (31%), "difficulty trusting others" (31%), "hard to ask for help" (29%), "difficulty finding someone trustworthy" (29%), "previous spiritual abuse" (15%), and "not committed to a local church" (8%).

Female Friendships

Nearly three-quarters (71%) reported having successful long-term relationships with other Christian women. Of the other 30%, the women reported these primary reasons: "don't feel like I fit in" (67%), "fear of rejection" (53%), "difficulty trusting" (46%), "fear of intimacy" (40%), "fear of vulnerability" (36%), and "fear of attraction" (35%). Lowest on the totem pole was having too high of expectations (24%). Nearly a third said they tend to avoid female friendships.

Sexual Identity Now

The women were then asked about changing to a heterosexual identity. Nine out of ten of the women (93%) said they have experienced at least some change. Of those, the largest group of respondents answered that they have experienced significant sexual identity change (37%). Only 8% said that they had experienced no change. At some point, it would be interesting to correlate their stated experience of change with the length of time and method of pursuing change.

The vast majority (98%) of the women answering my survey felt that their identity as a Christian woman had changed for the positive. Seven out of ten reported experiencing significant or better change of perspective.

When asked how they feel about being a woman now, two-thirds answered that they liked or thoroughly enjoyed being a woman. This result stands in dramatic contrast to how these women felt when growing up (nine out of ten ranged from ambivalent to greatly disliking the fact that they were female). One-quarter of the respondents (26%) marked the middle of a range of five, and 8% selected the two options closest to disliking being a woman.

Conclusion

The strongest findings among the 265 same-sex attracted women implicated the common thread of a painful childhood and abuse (91%). The common perspectives of the women seem to lead to external and then internal devaluing of key females and femininity during childhood demonstrated by a definite rejection of their mother as a role-model, a greater desire to emulate male role models, and the fact that before the age of 13 most felt somewhere between ambivalent to greatly disliking even being a girl.

External image and actions accompanied the inward beliefs of the women, evidenced by the fact that a vast majority considered themselves tomboys, that others had mistaken them for boys, and by their distrust of or hostility to men in general. The common issue of depression accompanied by alcoholism, drug use, or overeating seems to suggest an attempt to self-medicate. Perhaps one could consider lesbian relationships an attempt to self-medicate as well. Even the high rate of suicide attempts makes sense in light of the women's unresolved painful pasts.

Despite the painful events of their lives, these women were strongly motivated by personal religious belief to change orientation. After all, the top reason to pursue change almost unanimously cited was "relationship with God." This group of women was perhaps more committed to their local churches than the average Christian.

Most of the women (85%) were able to transition from a lesbian or bisexual identity to a heterosexual or ex-lesbian identity (81%) in an average of two and one-half years and commonly with the assistance of Exodus International and/or professional therapy. They were able to make a significant impact not only on their sexual identity but also on how they felt about themselves as women.

Finally, the collective information from this group of women strongly asserts not only that change is possible but that in a relatively brief amount of time, *significant* change can occur.

Suggested Reading and Resources

Throughout *Restoring Sexual Identity,* I have recommended various resources. Below I am including other tried and true titles from my own library you might find helpful:

A Strong Delusion, by Joe Dallas (Harvest House Publishers, 1996).

Healing Wounds of the Past by Don Schmierer (Promise Publishing, 2002). Don has also published other very helpful titles, *What's a Father to Do?* (Promise Publishing, 2000), and *An Ounce of Prevention: Preventing the Homosexual Condition in Today's Youth* (W Publishing Group, 1998).

Someone I Love Is Gay by Anita Worthen and Bob Davies (InterVarsity Press, 1996).

A Parent's Guide to Preventing Homosexuality by Joseph and Linda Nicolosi (InterVarsity Press, 2003). Dr. Joseph Nicolosi has also authored an excellent therapeutic book entitled, *Reparative Therapy of Male Homosexuality* (Jason Aronson Publishers, 1997).

Coming Out of Homosexuality by Bob Davies and Lori Rentzel (InterVarsity Press, 1994). Bob has authored a number of excellent books and articles about homosexuality as well.

Relationships by Drs. Les and Leslie Parrott (Zondervan, 2002).

The Power of Mother Love by Brenda Hunter (WaterBrook Press, 1999).

Love Won Out by John and Anne Paulk (Tyndale House Publishers, 1999).

Other books can be found at the following website specifically on the topic of homosexuality: www.regenbooks.org, the official Exodus online bookstore. Here you will find video, audio, and booklet materials addressing a number of related issues. Two especially useful resources are:

Roots of Lesbianism (video) by Starla Allen.

A Pastor's Guide to Ex-Gay Ministry (booklet) by Rev. Michael Riley.

Notes

Chapter 2: Where Does Same-Sex Attraction Come From?

1. A summary of my survey is in Appendix B.

2. Carla Golden, "Diversity and Variability in Women's Sexual Identities," in *Lesbian Psychologies: Explorations and Challenges,* Boston Lesbian Psychologies Collective, ed. (Chicago: University of Illinois Press, 1987), p. 19.

3. John Gallagher, "Gay for the Thrill of it," *The Advocate* (February 17, 1998).

4. Forty percent of the women in my survey believed at one point that they were born gay.

5. D. H. Hamer et al., "A Linkage between DNA Markers on the X-chromosome and Male Sexual Orientation," *Science* 261, no. 5119: pp. 321-27.

6. Philip Bereano, "The Irrelevance of the 'Gay Gene,'" *Seattle Times,* February 25, 1996. Reprinted in condensed form in *Professional Ethics Report,* vol. IX, no. 2 (Spring 1996).

7. George Rice et al., "Male Homosexuality: Absence of Linkage to Microsatellite Markers at Xq28," *Science,* vol. 284 (April 1999): p. 665.

8. A. Dean Byrd, Shirley E. Cox, and Jeffrey W. Robinson, "The Innate-Immutable Argument Finds No Basis in Science," *Salt Lake City Tribune,* May 27, 2001.

9. John Gallagher, "Gay for the Thrill of It," *The Advocate* (February 17, 1998).

10. John Arlidge, "No Tears for Passing of 'Gay Gene,'" *The Observer* (April 25, 1999).

11. D. McFadden and E.G. Pasanen, "Comparison of the Auditory Systems of Heterosexuals and Homosexuals: Click-Evoked Otoacoustic Emissions," *Proceedings of the National Academy of Sciences USA,* 95: pp. 2709-2713.

12. Ibid.

13. Paul Recer, "Researchers Find Difference in Gays," *The Associated Press* (March 2, 1998).

14. Ibid.

15. Ibid.

16. "Scientists Challenge Notion that Homosexuality's a Matter of Choice," *The Charlotte Observer,* August 9, 1998.

17. D. McFadden and H.S. Plattsmier, "Aspirin Abolishes Spontaneous Otoa-coustic Emissions," *Journal of Acoustical Society of America*, 76 (August, 1984): pp. 443-448.

18. D. McFadden, "Otoacoustic Emissions and Quinine Sulfate," *Journal of Acoustical Society of America*, 95 (June 1994): pp. 3460-74.

19. Ibid., 443.

20. McFadden and Plattsmier, "Aspirin Abolishes Spontaneous Otoacoustic Emissions," p. 443.

21. McFadden and Pasanen, "Comparison of the Auditory Systems of Hetero-sexuals and Homosexuals: Click-Evoked Otoacoustic Emissions," pp. 2709-2713.

22. Jeffrey Satinover, M.D., "The Gay Gene?" *The Journal of Human Sexuality*, (1996). The candid responses of some lesbian women in Miami, Florida reveal a certain common sense about the inner-ear study. Dorothy Acheson, a *Miami Herald* staff writer, wrote, "The inner-ear study generated a lot of discussion among local lesbians, with many of us brushing it off as 'poppy-cock,' in the words of one woman at a party over the weekend." In other words, the researchers are making quite a leap in logic to state that andro-gens (male hormones) were present in the womb to impact the formation of lesbians' ears. It is yet another leap to state that the androgens, if perhaps they were indeed present in greater number than in prenatal heterosexual women, impacted "an unknown" place in the women's brains that may just relate to sexuality. And yet another leap of faith to say that homosexuality in women is caused by the same dynamic that might have modified the cochlea.

23. McFadden and Pasanen, "Comparison of the Auditory Systems of Hetero-sexuals and Homosexuals: Click-Evoked Otoacoustic Emissions," pp. 2709-2713.

24. McFadden and Plattsmier, "Aspirin Abolishes Spontaneous Otoacoustic Emissions," p. 443.

25. S. Marc Breedlove et al., "Finger-Length Ratios and Sexual Orientation," *Nature*, vol. 404 (March 30, 2000): pp. 455-56.

26. Ibid.

27. Breedlove and Arnold, 1980, Tabibnia and Breedlove, 1997, Hegstrom and Breedlove, 1997.

28. www.ns.msu.edu/neurosci/people/faculty/breedlove.htm

29. Shawna Vogel, "Double Digit Discovery," ABC News.com, March 29, 2000.

30. Laurie Essig, "Lesbian Fingers," Mothers Who Think, Salon.com, October 16, 2000. Looking at the study from another perspective, Neil Whitehead, Ph.D., examined the statistical validity of the data and conclusions. The finger length study by Breedlove, Williams et al., "used a large number of interviewees. In such circumstances, although the mean finger lengths may be statistically different, they are often so close that it is not practically useful to say they are different. That is what happened in the present case."

Dr. Whitehead then reanalyzed the researcher's data concerning lesbian and heterosexual women and came to the conclusion that "there is obviously a very large overlap in the two populations, and although the two means may be statistically different, the difference is only 1 percent—which is a small effect, and not diagnostically useful in any sense." Whitehead also added that although "there are large numbers of *heterosexual* women who have much more 'masculine' finger-length ratios than most lesbians....This is not considered by the researchers to be related to their sexual orientation" (Neil Whitehead, "The New Finger-Length Study on Lesbians," NARTH website, July 24, 2001).

31. Jan Clausen, *Apples and Oranges* (Boston: Houghton Mifflin Company, 1999), xxvii.

32. Ibid., xxix.

33. Boston Lesbian Psychologies Collective, ed., *Lesbian Psychologies: Explorations and Challenges* (Chicago: University of Illinois Press, 1987), p. 4.

34. Ibid., p. 7.

35. Chris Bull, "Mom's Fault?" The Advocate.com, 2000.

36. Joe Dallas, *A Strong Delusion* (Eugene, OR: Harvest House Publishers, 1996), pp. 116-17.

37. Ibid.

Chapter 3: Classic Development of Lesbian Attraction

1. A summary of my survey is in Appendix B.

2. Merriam-Webster's Collegiate Dictionary Online, ©2002 Merriam-Webster, Incorporated.

3. Elizabeth Moberly, *Homosexuality: A New Christian Ethic* (Cambridge: James Clarke & Co., 1983).

4. Jan Clausen, *Apples and Oranges* (Boston: Houghton Mifflin Company, 1999), xvi.

5. Ibid., xvii.

6. Ibid., p. 40.

7. Ibid., p. 104.

8. Ibid., p. 125.

9. Ibid., p. 194.

10. Ibid., p. 222.

11. Definitions of abuse are classified in the summary in Appendix B.

12. J. Fieldman and T. Crespi, "Child Sexual Abuse: Offenders, Disclosure, and School-Based Initiatives," *Adolescence*, vol. 37, no.145: p. 151.

13. National Institute of Justice and Centers for Disease Control and Prevention, *Prevalence, Incidence, and Consequences of Violence Against Women Survey*, 1998.

14. Stanton Jones and Mark Yarhouse, *Homosexuality: The Use of Scientific Research in the Church's Moral Debate* (Downers Grove, IL: InterVarsity Press, 2000), p. 57.

15. Andrea J. Sedlak and Diane D. Broadhurst, *Executive Summary of the Third National Incidence Study of Child Abuse and Neglect* (U.S. Department of Health and Human Services, 1996).

16. Ibid.

17. Nancy Faulkner, "Pandora's Box: The Secrecy of Child Sexual Abuse," *Sexual Counseling Digest* (October 1996). Faulkner added,

> Finkelhor and Browne (1986) acknowledged that effects of the molestation may be delayed into adulthood. Long-term effects that are frequently reported and associated with sexual abuse include depression, self-destructive behavior, anxiety, feelings of isolation and stigma, poor self-esteem, difficulty in trusting others, tendency toward revictimization, substance abuse, and sexual maladjustment.

18. Rosie O'Donnell, *Find Me* (New York: Warner Books, 2002), p. 75.

19. Ibid, p. 6.

20. Ibid, p. 78.

21. Almost 20 percent of the women participating in my survey (on their experience overcoming lesbianism) reported having been sexually molested by another female. The largest defined group identified as female perpetrators was babysitters at more than 8 percent.

22. Jones and Yarhouse, *Homosexuality*, p. 57.

23. George Rekers et al., "Gender Identity Disorder," *The Journal of Human Sexuality* (1996). Originally published in *The Journal of Family and Culture*, vol. 2, no. 3, (1986).

24. Ibid.

25. Elaine V. Siegel, *Female Homosexuality: Choice Without Volition, a Psychoanalytic Study* (Hillsdale, NJ: The Analytic Press, 1988), xii.

26. Ibid., p. 3.

27. Ibid., xvii.

28. Ibid., p. 6.

29. J. Michael Bailey and Kenneth J. Zucker, "Childhood Sex-Typed Behavior and Sexual Orientation: A Conceptual Analysis and Quantitative Review," *Developmental Psychology*, 31 (1995): p. 49.

30. Jones and Yarhouse, *Homosexuality*, p. 52.

31. Ibid.

32. Siegal, *Female Homosexuality*, xvi.

33. Steven Donaldson, from a lecture given at the Evergreen Conference, 2002, Vancouver, Washington.

34. Siegal, *Female Homosexuality,* 219.

35. Donaldson, Evergreen Conference, 2002.

36. Siegel, *Female Homosexuality,* p. 219.

37. Ibid., p. 218.

38. Ibid., p. 221.

39. Bob Davies and Lori Rentzel, *Coming Out of Homosexuality: New Freedom for Men and Women* (Downers Grove: InterVarsity Press, 1993), p. 47.

Chapter 4: Healthy Female Gender Development

1. CNN Larry King Live, Interview with Lisa Beamer, aired December 24, 2001.

2. Steven Donaldson, from a lecture given at the Evergreen Conference, 2002, Vancouver, Washington.

3. Robert D. Wolgemuth, *She Calls Me Daddy* (Wheaton, IL: Tyndale House Publishers, 1996), p. 17.

4. Ibid., xi.

5. Focus on the Family's Physicians Resource Council, USA, *The Complete Book of Baby and Childcare* (Wheaton IL: Tyndale House Publishers, 1997), p. 353.

6. Ibid.

7. James Dobson, *Bringing Up Boys* (Downers Grove, IL: Tyndale House Publishers, 2001), p. 10.

8. Ibid., p. 11.

9. Neil and Briar Whitehead, *My Genes Made Me Do It!* (Lafayette, LA: Huntington House Publishers, 1999), p. 58.

10. Ibid., p. 59.

11. Ibid.

12. Wolgemuth, *She Calls Me Daddy,* p. 48.

13. Whitehead, *My Genes Made Me Do It!* p. 59.

14. Michael Gurian, *The Wonder of Girls* (New York: Simon and Schuster, 2002), p. 23.

Chapter 5: Establishing a Support System

1. Thanks to Ann Phillips, former Women's Ministry Director of Love in Action, Memphis, Tennessee, for this excellent suggestion.

2. "Policy Statement: Homosexuality and Adolescence," American Academy of Pediatrics, 1993.

3. Joseph Nicolosi, "Retrospective Self-Reporting of Changes in Homosexual Orientation: A Consumer Survey of Conversion Therapy Clients," *Psychology Reports,* 86 (2000): pp. 1071-88.

4. Steven Donaldson, from a lecture presented at the Evergreen Conference, 2002, Vancouver, Washington.

5. Mosaic Counseling Associates, "Tools for Finding a Good Counselor," www.mosaiccounseling.com.

6. W.E. Vine, *Vine's Complete Expository Dictionary of Old and New Testament Words* (Nashville, TN: Thomas Nelson Publishers, 1996), pp. 210, 545.

7. Bob Davies and Lori Rentzel, *Coming Out of Homosexuality* (Downers Grove, IL: InterVarsity Press, 1993), p. 26.

8. John and Anne Paulk, *Love Won Out* (Wheaton, IL: Tyndale House Publishers, 1999).

9. Mark A. Yarhouse and Lori A. Burkett, "An Inclusive Response to LGB and Conservative Religious Persons: The Case of Same-Sex Attraction and Behavior," *Professional Psychology: Research and Practice*, vol. 33, no. 3, (June 2002): pp. 235-241.

10. Robert Spitzer, "Subjects Who Claim to Have Benefited from Sexual Reorientation Therapy," Presented at the 2001 Annual Conference of the American Psychiatric Association.

11. Warren Throckmorton, "Initial Empirical and Clinical Findings Concerning the Change Process for Ex-Gays," *Professional Psychology: Research and Practice*, vol. 33, no. 3 (June 2002): pp. 242-48.

12. K.W. Schaeffer et al., "Religiously Motivated Sexual Orientation Change: A Follow-Up Study," *Journal of Psychology and Christianity*, 19 (1999): pp. 61-70.

Chapter 6: Healing from Abuse

1. Christine Sneeringer, "About Face," *Christian Single* (February 2001): p. 12.

2. Anne Paulk, *Study of Roots, Causes, and Treatment of Lesbianism*, 2001. See a summary of my survey in Appendix B.

3. To see the definitions used in the survey of each type of abuse, please refer to Appendix B.

4. Patricia Tjaden and Nancy Thoennes, "Prevalence, Incidence, and Consequences of Violence Against Women," National Institute of Justice and the Centers for Disease Control and Prevention (November 2000).

5. Table 2-9, Victimization Rates by Age, Sex, and Maltreatment Type, DCDC, The Administration for Children and Families, U.S. Department of Health and Human Services (1999).

6. "In Focus: The Risk and Prevention of Maltreatment of Children with Disabilities," National Clearinghouse on Child Abuse and Neglect, U.S. Department of Health and Human Services (February 2001).

7. Ibid.

8. Ibid.

9. *Prevention Pays: The Costs of Not Preventing Child Abuse and Neglect*, National Clearinghouse on Child Abuse and Neglect Information, U.S. Department

of Health and Human Services, updated April 19, 2002. For the individual studies mentioned in the quote, see below:

National Research Council, "Understanding Child Abuse and Neglect" (Washington, D.C.: National Academy Press, 1993).

C.S. Widom, "The Cycle of Violence" (Washington, D.C.: National Institute of Justice, 1992).

B.T. Kelley, T.P. Thornberry, and C. A. Smith, "In the Wake of Childhood Violence" (Washington D.C.: National Institute of Justice, 1997).

10. *Short- and Long-Term Consequences of Neglect,* National Clearinghouse on Child Abuse and Neglect Information, U.S. Department of Health and Human Services (updated April 6, 2001).

11. David Finkelhor, "Early- and Long-Term Effects of Child Sexual Abuse: An Update," *Professional Psychology: Research and Practice,* vol. 21, no. 5 (1990): pp. 325-30.

12. Nancy Faulkner, "Pandora's Box: The Secrecy of Child Sexual Abuse," *Sexual Counseling Digest* (October, 1996).

13. Chastity Bono, *The End of Innocence: A Memoir* (Irondale, AL: Advocate Books, 2002), p. 10.

14. Jan Frank, *A Door of Hope: Recognizing and Resolving the Pains of Your Past* (Nashville, TN: Thomas Nelson Publishers, revised 1995). p. 21.

15. Ibid., p. 48.

16. Ibid., p. 61.

17. Ibid., p. 71.

18. Ibid., p. 109.

19. W.E. Vine, *Vine's Complete Expository Dictionary of Old and New Testament Words* (Nashville, TN: Thomas Nelson Publishers, 1996), pp. 250-51.

Chapter 7: Overcoming Temptation

1. "Is This a Birth Defect?" www.crosswalk.com/experts/snyder.

2. "I Gave in to Temptation," www.crosswalk.com/experts/snyder.

3. Jane Boyer, from her testimony at Focus on the Family—Love Won Out conference, Philadelphia, PA, April 21, 2001.

4. A summary of my survey is in Appendix B.

5. W.E. Vine, *Vine's Complete Expository Dictionary of Old and New Testament Words* (Nashville, TN: Thomas Nelson Publishers, 1996), pp. 203-04.

6. Stephen Arterburn, Fred Stoeker, and Mike Yorkey, *Every Man's Battle: Winning the War on Sexual Temptation One Victory at a Time* (Colorado Springs: WaterBrook Press, 2000), p. 104.

7. Arterburn et al., *Every Man's Battle, p.* 159.

8. C.S. Lewis, *Mere Christianity,* pp. 124-125.

9. A summary of my survey is in Appendix B.

10. "Cybersex Addiction: Survey sees 'Health Hazard,'" *The Gazette*, May 6, 2000.

11. Kimberly S. Young, *Caught in the Net* (New York: John Wiley & Son, 1998), p. 27.

12. Stephen Watters, *Real Solutions for Overcoming Internet Addictions* (Ann Arbor, MI: Vine Books, 2001), p. 88.

13. Ted Roberts, *Pure Desire* (Ventura, CA: Regal Books, 1999), p. 32.

14. "Cybersex Addiction: Survey sees 'Health Hazard,'" *The Gazette*, May 6, 2000.

15. Arterburn et al., *Every Man's Battle*, p. 71.

16. Watters, *Real Solutions for Overcoming Internet Addictions*, 66. Patrick Carnes, *Out of the Shadows: Understanding Sexual Addiction* (Center City, MN: Hazelden Information Education, 1992), xiii.

17. Watters, *Real Solutions for Overcoming Internet Addictions*, p. 169.

Chapter 8: Healthy Female Friendships

1. Les and Leslie Parrott, *Relationships 101* (Tulsa, OK: Honor Books, 1998), p. 42.

2. Michael Haley, "Enduring Freedom," general address to the Exodus International 2002 Conference.

3. Brenda Hunter, *In the Company of Women*, (Sisters, OR: Multnomah Books, 1994), pp. 28-29.

4. Ibid., p. 76.

5. A summary of my survey is in Appendix B.

6. Bob Davies and Lori Rentzel, *Coming Out of Homosexuality: New Freedom for Men and Women* (Downers Grove: InterVarsity Press, 1993), p. 108.

7. A summary of my survey is in Appendix B.

8. Davies and Rentzel, *Coming Out of Homosexuality*, p. 108.

9. Lori Rentzel, *Emotional Dependency* (Downers Grove, IL: InterVarsity Press, 1990), p. 7.

10. Dee Brestin, *The Friendships of Women* (Wheaton, IL: Victor Books, 1988), p. 16.

11. A summary of my survey is in Appendix B.

12. Parrott and Parrott, *Relationships 101*, p. 23.

13. Ibid., p. 26.

14. Hunter, *In the Company of Women*, p. 133.

15. Ibid., p. 134.

16. Brestin, *The Friendships of Women*, p. 102.

17. Ibid., p. 91.

18. Hunter, *In the Company of Women*, p. 152.

19. Rentzel, *Emotional Dependency*, p. 9.

20. Hunter, *In the Company of Women*, p. 110.

Chapter 9: Men: Friendships, Singleness, and Marriage

1. George Santayana, quoted in Les and Leslie Parrott, *Relationships: How to Make Bad Relationships Better and Good Relationships Great* (Grand Rapids, MI: Zondervan, 1998) p. 69.

2. James Dobson, *Bringing Up Boys* (Downers Grove, IL: Tyndale House Publishers, 2001), pp. 19-20.

3. Michael Gurian and Jeremy Tarcher, *The Wonder of Boys* (New York: Penguin Putnam, 1996), p. 15.

4. Dobson, *Bringing Up Boys*, p. 25.

5. Gurian and Tarcher, *The Wonder of Boys*, p. 14.

6. Dobson, *Bringing Up Boys*, p. 25.

7. Ibid., p. 27.

8. Les and Leslie Parrott, *Relationships 101: How to Develop Intimacy with Those You Love* (Tulsa, OK: Honor Books, 1998), p. 53.

9. Quoted in Parrott and Parrott, *Relationships 101*, p. 55.

10. Parrott and Parrott, *Relationships 101*, p. 57.

11. Ibid., p. 54.

12. Don and Jan Frank, *Unclaimed Baggage* (Colorado Springs: NavPress, 2003).

13. Parrott and Parrott, *Relationships 101*, p. 58.

14. These tapes can also be ordered from www.christian-tapes.com or www.regenbooks.org.

15. Bob Davies with Lela Gilbert, *Portraits of Freedom: 14 People Who Came Out of Homosexuality* (Downers Grove, IL: InterVarsity Press, 2001), pp. 66-67.

Chapter 10: Parenthood and the Ex-gay Woman

1. Brenda Hunter, *In the Company of Women* (Sisters, OR: Multnomah Books, 1994), pp. 32-33.

2. Ibid., p. 33.

3. Brenda Hunter, *The Power of Mother Love* (Colorado Springs, CO: WaterBrook Press, 1997), xiii.

4. Hunter, *In the Company of Women*, p. 41.

5. Hunter, *The Power of Mother Love*, p. 26.

6. Ibid., p. 27.

7. Ibid.

8. Neil and Briar Whitehead, *My Genes Made Me Do It!* (Lafayette, LA: Huntington House Publishers, 1999), pp. 50-51.

9. Robert D. Wolgemuth, *She Calls Me Daddy* (Wheaton, IL: Tyndale House Publishers, 1996), p. 84.

10. Ibid., p. 90.

11. Daryl J. Bem, "Is EBE Theory Supported by the Evidence? Is It Androcentric? A Reply to Peplau et al.," *Psychological Review 105,* no. 2 (1998): p. 395.

12. Stanton Jones and Mark Yarhouse, *Homosexuality: The Use of Scientific Research in the Church's Moral Debate* (Downers Grove, IL: InterVarsity Press, 2000), p. 57.

13. Hunter, *In the Company of Women,* p. 41.

Anne Paulk may be reached
by writing to her at:

Anne Paulk
c/o Harvest House Publishers
990 Owen Loop North
Eugene, Oregon 97402

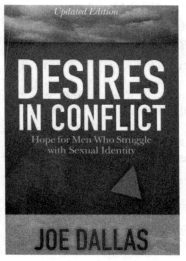

Desires in Conflict
(Revised edition)
Joe Dallas

For more than a decade, *Desires in Conflict* has been the definitive "must-read" for homosexuals wanting to change their lifestyle. Now, author Joe Dallas updates this all-important book to include new information and fresh insight into the increasingly debated subject of sexual orientation. This new edition will be welcome not only to men struggling with same-sex attraction, but to pastors, counselors, parents, family members, and friends searching for workable answers to the question "Can a homosexual change?"

I read *Desires in Conflict* for the first time when I was 19. I was fighting my own personal battle with homosexuality, sure that freedom wasn't possible and afraid that God and the Church hated me. More than a decade later, I am free of desires that once held me captive, strong in my faith, married to my amazing wife, Leslie, and currently the Executive Director of Exodus International, North America. The Lord used *Desires in Conflict* to shine a light into the darkness and to help guide me out of homosexuality. Joe Dallas has eternally impacted a generation of young people like me.

Alan Chambers
Executive Director
Exodus International, North America

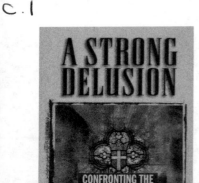

A Strong Delusion: Confronting the "Gay Christian" Movement

Joe Dallas

A Strong Delusion takes a powerful, straightforward look at the growing acceptance of homosexuality in the evangelical community. From his unique perspective of the pro-gay Christian movement, Joe Dallas provides:

- a thorough background in the development and nature of the movement

- a concise, detailed understanding of pro-gay theology's beliefs

- a clear biblical response to each belief

- a practical, compassionate plan to bring truth to people caught in the homosexual lifestyle

In *A Strong Delusion* you'll find the crucial balance between conviction and compassion and a practical guide to communicating with those who have embraced the pro-gay theology.